Will Men Be Like Gods?

AND

The Shadow on the Earth

WILL MEN BE LIKE GODS?

AND

THE SHADOW ON THE EARTH

Problems of Human Happiness I and II

By
OWEN FRANCIS DUDLEY

ST. AIDAN PRESS, LLC
Morning View, Kentucky

Will Men Be Like Gods? and The Shadow on the Earth: Problems of Human Happiness I and II.

Will Men Be Like Gods? Humanitarianism or Human Happiness?, first published in 1924 by Longmans, Green and Co., London, New York, Toronto. Reprinted from 1949 edition.

The Shadow on the Earth: A Tale of Tragedy and Triumph, first published in 1926 by Longmans, Green and Co., London, New York, Toronto. Reprinted from 1932 edition.

Typesetting, layout and cover design copyright 2023 St. Aidan Press, LLC.

Cover and title page ornament by Rebecca Read from Pixabay.

ISBN-13: 978-1-962503-00-6
ISBN-10: 1-962503-00-3

For more information, contact:
www.staidanpress.com
staidanpress@gmail.com

We have made no intentional change from the original text except to correct mistakes in spelling and punctuation.

For Mrs. Leanne Giese, née Arlinghaus
as a late wedding present
with many thanks for the loan of her copy
May God bless her in her new life

WILL MEN BE LIKE GODS?

Humanitarianism or Human Happiness?

INTRODUCED BY

G. K. CHESTERTON

PROBLEMS OF HUMAN HAPPINESS. I.

INTRODUCTION

IN WRITING a few prefatory words to Father Dudley's apt and spirited criticisms, I may be allowed rather to emphasize and expand one or two of his suggestions than to add anything to them. His book is concerned with a highly practical and even topical point in the controversies of the day. It is the question implied in the Utopias of Mr. H. G. Wells and in most of the new religions or new substitutes for religion. Father Dudley reviews all that humanitarianism which is so much connected with hedonism, and questions whether it is very much connected with happiness. Would the world even be happy, if it gave up all that has been counted holy? In this connection I would suggest only one query. The study of one of the Wellsian Utopias, or indeed of any other Utopias has often been interesting; but did anyone ever find it exhilarating? Does anyone feel those descriptions to glow in his memory like the real memories of human enjoyment? Does he, as Mr. Tony Weller said, feel his spirits rose; does he feel it half as much in the atmosphere of Utopia as in the atmosphere of a tavern with Mr. Tony Weller himself? There is something wanting in these ideals; and here the critic finds it in the very limitation of humanity to human things. It is all the more irreligious because it is a religion; that is, because it is taken seriously. Father Dudley practically identifies the humanitarianism of Wells with the humanity-worship of Comte. In this concentration he finds the key to its failure to produce happiness.

Perhaps the most interesting of the suggestions of Father Dudley, at least so far as I am concerned, is one that concerns the paradox of taking an irreligious humanity as a religion. It is actually much more difficult to worship a humanity that is not worshipping. So much of what is best in our race is bound up with its religious emotions and traditions, that to worship it without those intimations of the best would come very near to worshipping it at its worst. It is not so much that mankind is not enough as that mankind has never felt it enough to be enough. Man is maimed as well as limited by arresting those upward gestures that are so natural to him. Even if mankind could become such a mutual admiration society, men would in fact find each other less admirable. A self-contained and self-centred humanity would chill us in the same way as a self-contained and self-centred human being. For the spiritual hungers of humanity are never merely hungers for humanity. They are never merely aspirations for a completely humanised humanity, even as they exist in humanitarians. The proof of this is not peculiar to theology or even to religion; it is equally apparent in poetry and all imaginative arts. The child in the field, if left entirely to himself, does not merely wish to find the perfect parish ruled over by the perfect parish council. The child in the field wants to find fairyland; and that type of fancy must either be satisfied or thwarted; but it cannot be turned into something totally different. The poet does not merely wish to be with men; though the sanest sort of poet will wish this also on suitable occasions. But even the sanest sort of poet will often wish to be away from men and alone with something else. If he is a philosopher as well as a poet, he will probably want some intelligent identification of that something else; and if he looks for it, he will probably become a theologian as well as a philosopher. But even if he is only a poet, he will be haunted by something which is emphatically not human; and which he could really only rationally explain by calling it superhuman. In other words, it is impossible to turn all the eyes of that mutual admiration society inwards. Any number of their eyes always have been and always will be turned outwards, if only to a vague elemental environment of primeval mysteries and natural magic. To teach people to believe in God may be in its highest sense a hard task even among Christians. But to prevent people from thinking about God will be an impossible task even among agnostics; or perhaps especially among agnostics. It will be particularly impossible among agnostics who are also artists. If it has sometimes been difficult to keep the poet tied to home, it will be ten times more difficult to keep him tied to humanity. Comte, like Plato, will certainly have to expel poets from his Republic.

The other important part of the thesis, to my mind, concerns, not so much this paradox which is false, as another paradox which is true. It is the paradox that it is more possible to love men indirectly than to love them directly. There is such a thing as a passionate enthusiasm or tenderness for the ordinary man. But generally speaking it is rather an extraordinary man who feels it. Or, if this be not necessarily true, it is at least only felt by the ordinary man at extraordinary moments; that is, in extraordinary moods. Now if those moods and moments be sympathetically considered, I fancy it will always be found that they are what may be called mystical moods and moments. I mean that they are experiences in which the external manifestation of mankind seems to mean more than meets the eye; in which a crowd takes on a corporate character like a cloud; or in which a human face has the mask and the secret of a sphinx. Few are fired with a direct individual affection for the five people sitting on the other side of a railway-carriage; let us say a wealthy matron, given to snorting and sneering, a bright little Jew stockbroker, a large and vacant farmer, a pale and weary youth with a limp cigarette and a young woman perpetually powdering her nose. All these are sacred beings of equal value in the sight of God with the souls of Hildebrand and Shakespeare; but a man needs to be a little of a mystic to think so; or even to feel anything like it. In a vacuum of absolute agnosticism, in an utterly dry light of detached objectivity and positive knowledge, it is questionable whether he would feel it at all. If, as it is, he feels it occasionally and vaguely, it is really because he feels the remains of the old religious sentiment occasionally and vaguely. In the right mood he can still see a halo round humanity, because he still half-believes that humanity is half-divine. But that the stockbroker can be positively proved to be half-divine there is no proof. That the halo will in any case shine out of the interior of the fat farmer, by itself, and be visible to anybody anywhere, has never been scientifically demonstrated.

Now just as that vague hope that we call romance or poetry points to a paradise even if it be called elfland, so this vague charity or sense of sacred human values really points to a higher standard of sacredness. We have to look at men in a certain light in order to love them all; and the most agnostic of us know that it is not exactly identical with the light of common day. But the mystery is immediately explained when we turn towards that light itself; which is the light that lighteth every man that cometh into the world. Ordinary men find it difficult to love ordinary men; at least in an ordinary way. But ordinary men can love the love of ordinary men. They can love the lover of ordinary men, who loves them in an extraordinary way. It may be difficult to get a fat burgess and a fierce and hungry robber to love each other; but it is much easier to get them both to love St. Francis of Assisi for being able to love them both. And what is true of St. Francis is more true of his Divine model; men can admire perfect charity before they practise even imperfect charity; and that is by far the most practical way of getting them to practise it. It is not to leave men merely staring at each other and standing face to face to criticize and grow weary; it is rather to see them standing side by side and looking out together at a third thing; the world's desire and the love-affair of all humanity; which is really a human sun that can shine upon the evil and the good.

G. K. CHESTERTON.

Contents

WILL MEN BE LIKE GODS?

CHAPTER I

The Humanitarian Appeal

M EN DISLIKE being fooled. Men are in danger of being fooled today. And not merely fooled, but hoaxed. Not merely hoaxed, but utterly deceived. Men are in danger of staking their all upon what would prove to be the greatest delusion ever foisted on humanity, were it generally accepted. Men are being told that there is a certain road to human happiness in this world; that those who tread this road will find an Utopia of earthly bliss; that they will become "men like Gods." It is not the first time men have been so told. "You shall be as Gods," urged Satan in the Garden of Eden. But he lied. And the man and woman were fooled. So also will it be with the men and women who allow themselves to be caught in the snares of those who are repeating that invitation today. To expose those snares is the purpose of this book. We shall also make it our endeavour to prove that this road to Utopia is no road to human happiness, but to misery untold. There *is* a way to human happiness—one only way. We shall tell of that way later. This mystifying prelude must first unveil itself.

.   .   .   .   .

The world's present evil plight has drawn its attention to itself. The ensuing process of introspection is fostering a certain movement quietly and unobtrusively in our midst. Its name is *Humanitarianism*. It began in its modern form with Auguste Comte, some ninety years ago. Comte invented a human object of worship. Man, he said, should worship the "great being"—Humanity. Though the movement of Comte did not develop to any great extent, yet his idea remained. In England, Humanitarianism, as a positive philosophical system, has been ably expounded by positivists, such as Stuart Mill, Spencer, Huxley, and Tyndall. Its principles were popularised in 1886 by James Cotter Morison in a work entitled *The Service of Man*, described as "an essay towards the religion of the future." In a prefatory note the author writes: "The object of the book is to show how the Service of God, or of Gods, leads by natural evolution to the Service of Man; from Theolatry to Anthropolatry."

The appeal of Morison is to the reason and will of man that he shall put off belief in God and put on belief in Humanity. The *Civitas Dei* is a dream of the past, we must now strive to realise the *Regnum Hominis*. Many of the theological dogmas of Christianity, so he argues, are now felt to be morally repulsive by the more humane conscience of modern times. In the whole scheme of Christian redemption there are moral iniquities of which no good man of the present day would willingly be guilty himself. Christianity is hostile to morality in this world, for it offers salvation to a man who leads a life vile and injurious to society, and only repents at the last moment. It preaches salvation in the next world, not morality in this. The highest crown the Christian can win is that of martyrdom for his Faith; what benefit does this confer on men? The Christian principle is to regard pain and disease as trials sent by God: the true principle, the principle of science, is to fight and conquer them. The Christian works for a reward—for God in Heaven. Unalloyed altruism is higher. Only to his fellows can man be completely altruistic, "hoping for nothing again." The heavenward gaze is detrimental to Humanity. It takes man's mind off men. The Service of Man must be substituted for the Service of God. Thus James Cotter Morison.

And now today we have Mr. H. G. Wells before us as the avowed champion of Humanitarianism. When Mr. Wells wrote his *Outline of History*, he did it with a definite purpose. He intended to draw the attention of men to what he considers the true end of all human progress, the end towards which the human race is half-blindly, half-consciously struggling—the reign of universal happiness on earth; that glorious Utopia wherein men shall be like Gods. In his *Men Like Gods* (advertised in flaring letters in Oxford Street as advocating "No clothes, no marriage . . . ," which, no doubt, increased the sale), Mr. Wells pictures the Humanitarian Utopia actually attained. Man has found his freedom. He has conquered and won. He has boldly freed himself from the Christian superstition. He has found his happiness in the service of Man. Everybody is happy because everybody else is happy, each generation inheriting and adding to the happiness of the last. We can almost hear the applause of the babes yet unborn. We are left with a huge Mutual Admiration Society on earth. Thus Mr. H. G. Wells.

Now, curiously enough, Humanitarianism is being recruited at the present time from most unexpected quarters. For instance, Bolshevism is recruiting it, because ultimately it stands for the same principles and the same end. No doubt many Humanitarians would disown Bolshevism as too vulgar and violent, rather as we try to disown a vulgar relation; and yet in reality it is merely trying a short cut to their imagined Utopia. Bolshevism attempts to do away with the Christian religion and all belief in anything beyond this world. Religion is the opium of the people. It is in the way of Humanity. This is the only world that matters. Men must get everything they can in this world and spit at the next. Bolshevism is certainly successful in getting things. So far, however, it has not succeeded in *giving* very much, except misery, to Humanity. However, since its purpose is to put Man in place of God, Humanitarians should at least be grateful to it for supporting their own cause, however abrupt and violent the methods employed.

Again, in the non-Catholic religious world, we find Modernism lending its aid to the movement. What is the one perpetual theme of the Modernists? That Christianity must be made acceptable to the modern mind. Man's reason is the standard of truth. One by one the revealed truths of God are being thrown overboard. Christianity must be rationalised for the sake of man. The Modernists, all unconsciously perhaps, are putting man in place of God. And that is what Humanitarians want. Further, Protestantism as a whole is now being infected. It began with "Faith without works"; it is ending with "Works without Faith." The shibboleth of today is: "It does not matter what a man believes, it is what he does that matters. Give me a man who lives for his fellow-men! That's Christianity!" In other words, God's Revealed Truth, and therefore God, comes second. Man comes first.

We find, too, that modern social reformers and philanthropists outside the Catholic Church take it for granted that the first and last end of Christianity is the improvement of social conditions. Without entering upon an argument with the "Humanitarian Christians," we would like to remind them that it is useless to try and square Christianity with Humanitarianism. The two are contradictories. They are aiming at opposite ends. We would remind them, too, that Christ did not make His Church a mere philanthropical society. Christianity does not exist to establish man in security and prosperity on earth. Its purpose is to establish the Kingdom of God on earth. Material prosperity may, and in a general way does, follow accidentally when the laws of the Kingdom of God are obeyed. It is also a matter of fact that the Catholic Church has done more for humanity than all the Humanitarians put together. But that is by the way. What we wish to emphasize is that the object of Christianity is to put men in possession not of the things of this world, but of the things of Heaven; and to lead them to their final end, eternal union with God. Seeing that the object of Humanitarianism is to turn men from their final end to this world as an end in itself, it is clear that you cannot be a Humanitarian and a Christian at the same time. And the real genuine full-fledged Humanitarian recognises this. He knows that Christianity stands for something quite different from what he stands for. The real Humanitarian is a positivist. He tells you frankly that we must confine ourselves to the positive facts of physical science. We must rid ourselves of all supernatural religion. Physical science cannot discover God. We must not worry as to whether there is a God or not. God does not matter. Leave God alone. Leave Eternity alone. Leave the next world alone. Even if there is a next world it does not concern us. This is the world that matters. Heaven is a dream. This world is a fact. We must therefore confine our attention to *it*.

We have given, then, a rough sketch of the aims and end in view of the Humanitarian movement. Men by their own efforts are to establish the Kingdom of Man on earth, the reign of universal happiness. Man is to be his own saviour. The Saviour of men is to be ousted from the position He has held for nigh upon two thousand years. The Kingdom of Man is to take the place of the Kingdom of God.

Now we admit that at first glance the Humanitarian Utopia appears rather attractive. From a worldly standpoint it would be wonderful if all men could be scientifically trained without bothering about religion; trained to live for one another and to love one another to such an extent that all selfishness would vanish. It would be a glorious thing if the petty self-interests of individuals and nations could sink into an abyss of shame before the great ideals of Goodness, Beauty, and Truth. In the Humanitarian scheme men would be scientifically educated in the pursuit of those ideals. The "Highest Good" of Humanity would be held like a flaming torch of glory before the eyes of every man, woman and child. Against suffering and pain and all the apparent brutalities of Nature, man, trained to the finger-tips, would wage a ceaseless warfare. All that hurt the individual or harmed society would be ruthlessly cut down by an army of Eugenists. No longer would men weep and whine beneath the Cross of Christ. Christianity has taught men to accept suffering. They shall now be taught to resist it and conquer. No longer shall men be martyred for the Faith of Christ, for Faith shall be no more. For nigh upon two thousand years men have been enslaved by the Christian superstition. Humanity's childhood was held in bondage by priest and Pope. They told it fairy-tales. But Humanity is growing up—thinking for itself. It has reached the age of reason. The priests must know their day is done. Men must learn the truth. What good is God, Who hides His face in silence? Look at the world! Look at its wars! Look at its cruelties! Look at its disease and pain! What does the God of the Christians care? Is He all-powerful? Then what has He done? The wailing of Humanity has reached the vaults of Heaven and echoed back unheard. No, Humanity is now awaking from its dream. No longer shall it trust in God, but trust in Man it *shall*. And Man shall win where God has failed. This world of men shall set the world aright. No God shall interfere. Science shall teach all men to know themselves, to know their powers, to know how wonderful they are. Men shall create a new God in their own image and likeness. Humanity shall be their God!

That is the Humanitarian appeal.

CHAPTER II

The Humanitarian Hoax

FROM A WORLDLY standpoint the Humanitarian appeal is very seductive. Many are listening to it who have become indifferent to Christianity. It is intruding itself whenever and wherever it can find expression: in the press, in novels, in "Higher Thought," in Christian Science, in pseudo-Science, in pseudo-psychology, in pseudo-Eugenics, and in pseudo-Christianity. Many are yielding to its seductions. Many are wavering; for many must pause on the brink and shiver who realise what accepting the full Humanitarian creed involves. It involves a complete burning of boats. It means deliberately disowning any responsibility to a Personal God and, instead, owning yourself responsible solely to your fellow-men. It means putting Man in place of God. It is ultimately that deliberate defiance of God so clearly portrayed in a recent Humanitarian work called *Light*. It is the supreme revolt of the rational creature against His Creator. It is transferring to Man what is due to God. It is idolatry. And let no man be deluded because the exponents of Humanitarianism so often couch their theme in such moderate language and make their appeal in so reasonable a manner. The end to be attained is exactly the same whether urged in the quiet tones of a Morison or in the shrill blasphemies of *Light*.

Before exposing the falsity of the Humanitarian arguments, we would like to suggest the following questions:—What would

Humanity be like in a Godless Utopia? Would men really find
Humanity worth worshipping, a Humanity that had turned
away from all hopes and aspirations outside itself; a Humanity
supposedly entrapped by some blind force in this fragment of
the universe, chained to this earth—an earth once called the
vale of tears and yet the floor of Heaven, but now become a
dungeon-cell? Would men really attempt to live the moral life
which, as Humanitarians admit, is necessary for happiness?
Would they really strive for an abstract idea of the "Highest
Good" without a belief in God, with no eternity ahead? Even if
this were possible, even if all that is inimical to social welfare
were removed, even if every man had all this world could give,
would happiness be then attained? Would Humanity be happy
in its own homage and service? Could it bring forth from its
own womb the happiness for which men crave? If not, then men
would turn and rend their God!

We venture to suggest that Humanitarianism will lead men
into a stupendous hoax; for its imaginary Utopia is based, all
unconsciously perhaps, on the negative conditions of happiness, not on its positive materials. Happiness is not necessarily attained when all that is not consistent with it is removed.
These will-o'-the-wispers have yet to discover what happiness
is in itself. They ignore the claim of all the millions of Christians, from the time of Christ and onwards to the present day,
that happiness is within and not without. The unvarying spiritual experience of two thousand years has taught a vast body
of men that real happiness can only come from the union of
the soul with God, that it does not depend on outward circumstances. Their consentient and consistent witness to this experience is a simple historical fact. The Humanitarians sneer at
Christianity as a myth; but the "myth" has actually produced
what they have yet to find, and what in their way, according to
all the past experience of men, they never will find. What kind

of happiness would any rational being find in working solely for a Humanity doomed to extinction? For the extinction of human life on earth is scientifically a matter of time. Of what value would be all the moral efforts of all the individuals in the world, if the fruits of all those efforts were fated to fade like a shadowy pageant, leaving no trace behind?

We venture to suggest that the last state of Humanity, its life stripped of all abiding value, would be worse than the first; a state of dull despair. Its final condition might well be that predicted in the *Dunciad* of Pope:

> "Religion, blushing, veils her sacred fires,
> And unawares Morality expires.
> Nor public flame, nor private dares to shine;
> Nor human spark is left, nor glimpse divine!
> Lo! thy dread empire, Chaos, is restor'd;
> Light dies before thy uncreating word:
> Thy hand, great Anarch! lets the curtain fall;
> And universal darkness buries all."

CHAPTER III

The Dethronement of Reason

THE INTRODUCTION of this chapter is necessary in order that we may understand what underlies Humanitarian thought. It is the only one in the book which concerns itself with technical philosophy. A study of its brief contents will certainly do no harm, and may even be of profit to those who enjoy the exercise of reason. Those who do not would be wiser to pass on to Chapter IV.

We have already shown how the advocates of Humanitarianism rest their doctrines on the basis of Positivism. It is our purpose here to undermine that basis by exposing the falsity of the Positivist way of thinking. We shall set forth the basic doctrines of Positivism as briefly as possible and, to save repetition, deal with them one by one as we present them. We do not intend to give the philosophical arguments for the existence of God, or for the existence and immortality of the soul. These can be studied in the innumerable works of Catholic philosophers. We intend to expose Positivistic Humanitarianism merely to the extent of exhibiting the folly of those who put their trust in it.

In the first place Positivism is an attempt to confine the human mind exclusively to the positive facts of physical science: to the truths of mathematics, astronomy, physics, chemistry, biology and sociology, and this to the exclusion of metaphysics and theology. Only facts which are accessible to observation by the senses are the object and criterion of knowledge. The knowable is thus identified with the sensible. Since God is not among the positive facts of physical science, the enquiry into His existence or non-existence is useless and irrelevant to mankind. In practice the existence of God is to be ignored as unknowable.

And Positivists are quite consistent in ignoring God, seeing that for them only the sensible is the object of knowledge. If their philosophy is true, then it is a waste of breath to argue about the existence of God as the First Cause of all things. To them a "cause" is merely that which is perceived by our senses as regularly preceding anything, not, as we should teach, "that which makes a thing to be what it is," i.e., that which confers being. Positivism maintains that, since the senses cannot perceive the notion of causality, causality is a mere word, nothing more. Hence the road to all arguments for the existence of a First Cause is blocked at the entrance. It is, therefore, that very dogmatic assertion that we can only know in one way, by way of the senses, that first needs our attention.

Do we know by the senses alone? Sensible experience undoubtedly supplies us with the primary material of all our knowledge. But after receiving this primary material what do we do with it? Are we content with so many sensations and nothing more? A mere accumulation of sensible experiences? A mere picture-gallery of images? No, most certainly not. On examination we find that we make use of this empirically acquired material. We abstract ideas from the concrete. And we disengage these ideas from their material setting. These abstract ideas are quite distinct and quite different from pictures formed in the imagination. For instance, I could not ask my grocer for a piece of *fresh* bacon, unless I had an abstract idea of *freshness* which is distinct from all the images of all the pieces of bacon I have ever seen. It is obvious, too, that our senses have not the power to form these abstract ideas. Our senses can only perceive the sensible qualities of a thing. This process of abstraction is the work of the mind, not of the senses. How do we know that? Because every object perceived by the senses is a material thing determined by certain particularising notes, e.g., so much quantity, such and such a quality. We are conscious, however, of having cognitions other than these; cognitions in which the object is stripped of these particularising notes, i.e., abstract ideas. There must be, then, a faculty, distinct from the faculty of sense, which does this work of stripping or abstracting. We call this faculty the *intellect*— the faculty which uses as its instrument the brain.

And it is here, we think, that Positivists of the sensationalist school of thought go astray. They fail to perceive that the faculty of intellect is distinct from the faculty of sense. Hence their further failure to perceive that the intellect *knows* things which the senses cannot know. They have, as it were, shut themselves up in a box by flatly refusing to admit any knowledge other than sense-knowledge. They have pulled the lid down upon themselves and latched it fast. That is the explanation of their error. That is why the abstract ideas formed by the intellect do not constitute real knowledge for them. And yet it is as clear as daylight, when we look into our consciousness, that we have abstract ideas and real knowledge derived from them. Are not such ideas as goodness, justice, love, realities? Men prove that they are by pursuing them. Our intellect can no more escape from these ideas than the eye can escape from seeing things.

The very essence then, so it seems to us, of the Positivists' error is this: *it is a refusal to accept the dictates of conscious experience.* Their whole system of philosophy is thus vitiated at its very source. They have cut themselves off from vast realms of knowledge. The whole kingdom of inner realities is closed. For the senses cannot produce abstract ideas. To them the notion of the abstract is a chimera. The ideas of substance or being (i.e., the innermost reality of things), causality, the universal, are words, no more. The particular sciences, which are their forage-ground, stop short before the enquiry into the fundamental problems. And, since Positivists refuse to recognise the science which fearlessly institutes that enquiry, we mean metaphysics, they are limited to the shallows of knowledge.

Metaphysics has for its object the abstract. It is the science which gazes upon the being itself of things. The metaphysician can launch out into the deep, into the innermost principles of nature and thought, into the ultimate causes of existence, into the ultimate realities. The particular sciences, such as physics, mathematics, chemistry, biology, all add their quota to thought and knowledge, but it is left to metaphysics to make a synthesis of the knowledge acquired. We would like here to note a curious fact. Positivists, although they affirm the metaphysical world unknowable, yet argue about it. How could they do even that much without representing it to themselves first? The Positivist thinker, who once accused the writer of being guilty of a "metaphysical error," must have had some idea of a metaphysical world to be able to make the accusation. Even more, surely Positivists, who proclaim the doctrines of monism and evolutionism, are actually presenting a metaphysic of their own! Monism stands for the unity of composition in beings, evolutionism for their oneness of origin. Surely *unity* or *oneness* are abstract metaphysical ideas! The plain truth is that you cannot escape metaphysics.

Now, lest we become wearisome, we will broach what we have been leading up to. We have seen that the intellect can apprehend what the senses cannot. Amongst the primary apprehensions of the intellect are the notions of *being*, and of *cause*. *Being* is *that which is, that which exists. Cause* is *that which makes a thing to be what it is, that which confers being*. On these two notions rests what Kant called the cosmological argument for the existence of God. The intellect also perceives the close relation of *cause* to *being,* when it perceives the self-evident *principle of causality.* This principle may be expressed thus: "All contingent being must have a cause." By contingent being we mean that which is capable of non-existence. We will bring this philosophical excursion to an end by indicating how the intellect can reason out the existence of God with the aid of this principle of causality.

It is manifest that things which exist in this universe are capable of non-existence; for we see things come into existence and pass out of it. But things which are capable of non-existence do not exist of necessity. There is no absolute need for them to exist. I can lay my finger on one thing after another and say, "there is no need for this to exist." And yet these things *do* exist. Now the principle of causality tells me that things which are capable of non-existence must have a cause, something which confers their being. These things cannot come into existence of themselves out of nothing. That would be unthinkable. Therefore something must have caused their existence. And that something must be absolutely necessary to their existence, otherwise they would not exist. In other words, the existence of contingent beings cannot be explained without the existence of a necessary being. And just as contingent beings are not self-existent, so also a necessary being *is* self-existent. That Necessary, Self-existent Being is God. We may add two corollaries: (1) If God did not exist, then nothing would exist. (2) Since things do exist, therefore God exists.

To sum up what has been said. The human mind cannot be confined to the positive facts of physical science, for, even when gauging the external, it reaches far beyond the bounds of sense-perception. Still more does it penetrate into the inner realities of things. Unless self-chained like the Positivist mind, it instinctively delves deep down into the metaphysical world and finds—God. As we unmask Positivism we find it to be but a system enslaving its adherents to the superficialities of the age. To proclaim the existence of the Infinite Being unknowable because undiscoverable by the microscope or by the other means of physical science is mere puerility. We might as well expect to discover the stars by means of a cookery-book. The system which confines knowledge to the senses is not worthy of the name of philosophy. It contradicts true philosophy.

Its acceptance involves, consciously or unconsciously, intellectual suicide.

Chapter IV

The Enthronement of Man

W E NOW COME to the question of the influence of Positivism and of its relation to Humanitarianism. Why has it been so successful in moulding, directly or indirectly, the minds of millions, in spite of its manifest superficialities? What is the secret of its power? If the Positivist way of thinking (or of not thinking) were confined to the comparatively small number of its philosophical exponents, it would not matter so much. We should look upon these enthusiasts as so many unfortunates enclosed in the box of their senses, not meriting serious attention. But, unhappily, vast numbers of people are, all unwittingly, surrendering to the seductions of these sophistries, the influence of which is largely responsible for the general decay of religion which we are witnessing today. The masses are not, of course, interested in the philosophical teaching of Positivism, but they are intensely interested in the consequences of that teaching. Why are the writings of Mr. H. G. Wells so popular? He has a clever and absorbingly interesting way of writing, it is true. But is that the only secret of his hold on the popular mind? We think not. We think his power lies even more in this: he is giving people what they want. That the masses in England are drifting into paganism is a truism. But whether they are quite comfortable in conscience about doing so is a matter of doubt. They read authors such as Mr. Wells and find the road to irreligion made smooth and their qualms laid low. They learn that progress in human knowledge seals the doom of religion and that the death of Christianity is but a matter of time. Christianity passes like all else. Humanitarianism will take its place.

Herein, we think, lies the secret of the influence of Positivism. It offers a substitute for what it would take away, Humanity as a substitute for God. And it argues so glibly for that substitute. Religion is now seen to be but an anthropomorphic interpretation of the universe, justified perhaps at the outset by the necessity of securing some initial ideals for mankind. Gradually, however, it has been forced to make way for a scientific, objective, Positivistic mode of thought which will obtain complete victory in the end. Thus the religion that is left today is but a survival from the past. This theory rests on Comte's famous "Law of Three Stages." Comte maintained that there is a stage in human knowledge when we give a "theological" explanation of things by assigning them to a supernatural agency; we then give a "metaphysical," and finally a "positive" explanation, associating phenomena together according to laws. With the advance of knowledge religion will take a back place and finally disappear; it will vanish like smoke in the air. God will go.

But, if God is no longer to be worshipped, some object of worship must take His place; for man inevitably tends to worship. Clearly that object of devotion should be Man himself—the highest product of Nature. Humanity-worship is a logical consequence of the principles of Positivism, as its leading exponents have so clearly recognised. A substitute must be given for what is taken away. And Comte, as the founder of Positivism, was not foolish but quite consistent in proclaiming himself the first pontiff of the religion of Humanity. It is true that some of his followers, led by Emile Littré, were somewhat shy of the new cult and professedly accepted Positivism in its scientific aspect alone. Littré declared, however, that the true end of man was to work for the progress of humanity by studying, loving, and enriching it; and surely to make devotion to the human race the end of man comes very near to the worship of Humanity. In the broad sense to worship Humanity means to acknowledge it as the supreme object of our attention and devotion. Comte's system of "sacraments" and ceremonies is not the essential of that worship. The more orthodox followers of Comte, led by Pierre Laffitte, accepted the full cult of Positivism, as well as its philosophical system. Frederic Harrison, James Cotter Morison, and others imbued with the ideals of Comte have striven for the cause of Humanitarianism in England. And they have not toiled in vain. What Harrison calls "our faith" and "the Human Religion" is making rapid way in our midst. Morison seems to see his vision realised already. He exclaims, somewhat prematurely, "Thus the worship of deities has passed into the 'Service of Man.' Instead of Theolatry, we have Anthropolatry. The divine service has become human service."

The issues, then, are clear. Men are now faced by the choice of two offers. Humanitarianism is the one offer, Christianity is the other. By "Christianity" we mean true Christianity—Catholicism. As a form of Christianity, Protestantism scarcely counts today in the world of thought. Its Christian doctrines are watered down to the point of insipidity. At its best it has but a jumble of contradictory opinions to offer. Divisions have more or less nullified whatever influence it may have had in the past. Even the reunion movement is a part-attempt to close up the ranks in face of danger. Not only this, but thousands are feebly surrendering to the enemy. Even now Protestantism is honeycombed with Humanitarian thought. Its very foundations are being sapped away. But the Catholic Church stands before the world undivided, unmoved, unashamed, and unafraid. Hated by her enemies and loved by her children, she compels the attention of men. Old, but amazingly alive, she refuses to die. She does not even wear the seal of doom upon her brow. She says she cannot die. She stands there like a rock. The Catholic Church is a power to be reckoned with. And the Humanitarian instinctively recognises her as the enemy. Mr. Wells in his *Men Like Gods* significantly chose, not a Protestant clergyman, but a Catholic priest, to represent the Christian religion as the enemy of his Utopia. The representation was childish, but its meaning was quite clear. Mr. Wells was quite right in choosing a Catholic priest. The Catholic Church and Humanitarianism are deadly enemies. They each stand for what the other hates. One stands for the Worship of God, the other for the Worship of Man. They each offer what the other rejects.

One offers the Kingdom of God, the other the Kingdom of Man.

Chapter V

The Humours of Utopia

W E EXAMINED in a previous chapter the basis on which Humanitarianism rests—the basis of a false system of philosophy commonly called Positivism. A building that rests on a rotten foundation is not likely to be very reliable in its upper stories. It is therefore a matter of common prudence that the dazzling Utopia which crowns the Humanitarian edifice should be put to the test of critical examination. Will it stand the test, or will it prove to be constructed of so much flimsy tinsel? The devotees of Humanity bid us go and sell all that we have for the sake of this Utopia on earth offered in exchange for the Kingdom of Heaven. The fool will jump at the glittering bait. The wise man will pause and consider.

We have seen how, in the Humanitarian scheme, Christianity is to go and a new order to take its place. In this new order the place of Christian moral teaching is to be taken by the scientific morality of social utilitarianism. Man's worldly well-being is to be the sole motive-force of all our actions and the ultimate criterion of morality. Man must be scientifically trained to conform his actions to the welfare of the community. When he acts thus his actions are morally good. Actions harmful to the community are morally bad. In the Humanitarian Utopia each man's happiness is bound up in the happiness of all the rest. The amelioration of humanity, therefore, must be our ceaseless pursuit. We must perpetually strive for social happiness. Everything injurious to that happiness must be weeded out. Thus will the new order be attained. Mr. Marshall Gauvin, writing in *The Literary Guide*, says:

> "A new ideal stands at the door of the human heart. It is the ideal of a salvation that can be realised in this world. This world, and not another, is man's home. This life, and not another, is man's supreme concern. . . . The heaven that is to be will be in this world, when humanity comes to enjoy enlightened freedom, blessed with truth and crowned with love."

And Mr. Wells has drawn a vivid picture of this new order realised in the Utopia of his visions. In his *Men Like Gods* he leads us into the Promised Land of human desires—a wonderful world wherein all that men seek is found, and all that men dream is fulfilled. There has been a systematic training of the race in scientific morality. The worship of God has gone. The inhabitants of Utopia are freed from all "the lies of dogmatic religion and dogmatic morality." The marriage bond is a thing of the past. Free-love reigns supreme. It is recognised that man is fundamentally an animal, that his appetites must be satisfied and his instincts released. These children of light have taken hold, soul and body, of the life and destiny of the race. By a scientific elimination of almost all that is unpleasant and distressing, a maximum of physical ease and comfort has been secured. Everything goes without a hitch. The eye and the ear are at peace. Even dogs have given up barking. Whether this has been accomplished by breeding non-barkers or by the tuning-up of all dogs to the Utopian level, Mr. Wells does not say. There has also been a great cleansing of the world from "noxious insects, from weeds and vermin and hostile beasts." Even Dr. Saleeby, the great Eugenist, would be satisfied with the precautions taken against disease-carriers. We read: "The attack upon the flies had involved the virtual rebuilding of a large proportion of Utopian houses and a minute cleansing of them all throughout the planet."

And, glory be to the Goddess Eugenia, there has been "a certain deliberate elimination of ugly, malignant, narrow, stupid and gloomy types" of men and women. The standard of beauty required for Utopia is not actually specified, but we take it that the number of unsuccessful candidates has been considerable. There are "no really defective people in Utopia." Only the fittest and finest have survived. Stark Apollos wander to and fro in Olympian nudity, marvels of grace and physical splendour. These beautiful creatures move about their Garden of Eden absorbed in the task of installing the latest improvements. Soliloquising in the person of one of his characters, Mr. Wells exuberantly exclaims: "Life marched here; it was terrifying to think with what strides. . . . And pervading it all must be the happy sense that it mattered; it went on to endless consequences." Towards what it marched, why it mattered, and what the endless consequences were, we cannot discover. Mr. Wells and his Utopians seem to be equally in the dark. The future is left hazy in a smoke-screen of rhetoric. In a final vision we are bidden to note the Humanitarian movement even now progressing in this world: "the Great Revolution that is afoot on earth; that marches and will never desist nor rest again until old Earth is one city and Utopia set up therein." The day is coming when men will "laugh at the things they had feared, and brush aside the impostures that had overawed them"; when the "Sons of Earth . . . would go proudly about their conquered planet and lift their daring to the stars."

That is, then, a vision of the new order which is to replace the Christian order. And it represents very adequately the imagined fulfilment of Humanitarian hopes. We do not mean to be profane, but we must say that Mr. Wells' solemn description of Utopia strikes us as irresistibly funny. We are not surprised that one of the Worldlings who visited Utopia was found to be several inches longer on his return to Earth, evidently the result of swallowing such a tall story. These Gods and Goddesses, strutting about their Wonderland, doing their tremendous work of making it more and more comfortable and pleasant to live in, are really very funny people. They take themselves and their solemn task so seriously. But why? What is it all for? Why all this fuss? Why is everybody being made so comfortable and fit and beautiful? For what purpose is this world of men being made so perfect? If I go into an engine-shed and see an engine being polished up and oiled, the nuts being tightened, defective parts repaired, weak bearings replaced, and the whole mechanism put in perfect working order, I immediately understand why it is being done. The engine is going to do a journey to some definite place. The mechanics who are doing the job do not strike me as being funny. They know why they are doing it. But these wonderful Utopians do not know why they are making so much ado about their world and working it up to such a pitch of perfection. A Humanitarian dare not answer: "They are doing it for themselves." He *would* answer: "They are doing it for the next generation." But that is what the last generation said, and that is what the next generation will say, and the generation after that. I want to know the final purpose of it all, the final end. To work without a real goal in view is folly. What good can all this hubbub serve when each generation knows that it, and each succeeding generation in turn, will become extinct? Moreover, these Utopians not only do not know where their world of Humanity is going, but they don't know why it is going. The only thing they do know is that they and their planet may stop going. But what matter as long as there is "progress"? Onwards! Onwards! Onwards!

And Mr. Wells invites us, nay, storms at us, to emulate these mad 'bus-drivers careering wildly ahead, why and whither they know not! It is difficult to believe that the future generations of the human race will ever sink to such depths of imbecility. I sincerely hope these "Men like Gods" will be like "gods." I sincerely hope they will be myths. If we refuse to be carried away by the rhetoric of Mr. Wells and probe beneath the surface of his visionary Utopia, we shall perceive that its realisation is supremely unlikely. Whether Humanitarians, carrying all before them, could achieve another kind of Utopia, very different from that of their aspirations, is another question. If so, it would prove no Eden of happiness, but an ash-heap of dead hopes and disillusionments. But that is by the way. In criticising so ruthlessly this ideal world of Mr. Wells and other Humanitarians we have incurred the onus of justifying that criticism. Why do we consider the attainment of this de-Christianised order of perfection so unlikely? Can it be shown that the whole theory of social utilitarianism is fallacious through and through, from beginning to end; that, as Positivism is essentially a refusal to face the facts of conscious experience, so also is Humanitarianism essentially a refusal to face the facts of life?

We shall proceed forthwith to the task which we undertook in writing this book—the highly congenial task of exploding the Humanitarian Utopia.

CHAPTER VI

The Goodness of the Godless

THE SALIENT feature of the utilitarian scheme of the Humanitarians is the general happiness of mankind on earth, which they urge us to seek as the supreme end of human life, and in which is supposedly bound up the happiness of each one of us.

Confronted by that appeal my mind naturally responds with the query: "What *is* this general happiness of mankind for which I am asked to strive?" If I am to make the happiness of others the directing force of my conduct in life as well as the principle of my own happiness, I must first know in what the happiness of others consists. Social happiness is obviously the happiness of so many individuals. I find on examination that happiness is essentially relative to the individual person and varies in each case. The happiness of one person is not the happiness of another. Thus at the offset I am faced by the difficulty of not knowing at what I am aiming. What sort of happiness shall I secure for others? And what sort of happiness will others secure for me? We cannot all make each other happy in our own way. Each man can, or can try to, make himself happy in his own way. That is all. Humanitarians, then, are asking us to aim at a collective happiness for men before they can tell us in what it consists. And if each man's happiness is really bound up in the happiness of all the rest, in the knowledge of the happiness of others, then, at its best, this Utopian happiness would mean: "I am happy because you are happy that I am happy." Could any rational being mistake such a transparent absurdity for the happiness of Humanity?

At this juncture the enthusiasts of the vogue we are considering would probably urge that the highest forms of human happiness can be produced by the faithful pursuit of truth, kindness, love, and, above all, of pure altruism, without any aid from religion. But surely to disconnect these ideals from religion is to rob them of all reality. Human nature is ever demanding an answer to the question: "Why should I be good? Why should I be true? Why should I love?" To reply merely: "For the sake of Humanity" is to prompt a further query: "Why for the sake of Humanity?" Under what obligation am I to be good for the sake of Humanity? What absolute or obligatory value can Humanity give to morality isolated from religion? Humanitarians proclaim to me a moral imperative which, put to the test, reduces itself to an empty vaunt. From whom would they, any more than our modern rationalists and materialists, obtain authority to make and execute moral laws in the Godless world of their dreams—moral laws without which all organised society would be reduced to chaos? They deny any authority derived from God. Do they expect to derive moral authority from themselves?

These irreligionists are powerless to enforce what they perceive to be necessary. Their "morality," moreover, being confined within the narrow limitations of space and time, is stripped of all permanent value; for its end is foreseen with the death of the human race on earth. Humanitarians cannot even offer me a serious inducement to lead a moral life.

And these very people are today setting forth with a great beating of drums to imbue the world with their notion of "morality" for the ousting of Christian moral teaching. Mr. F. J. Gould, writing in *The Literary Guide*, declares: "Humanist forces, gradually accumulating and co-operating all over the world, will evolve an International of Education, with a front as resolute, with banners as proud, with resources as solid, as the International of the Cross; . . ." They may succeed in "educating" the unthinking, but a very low intellectual level must be reached before the majority of men are gulled into accepting "moral laws" which carry with them no sanction or obligation. The folly of looking for morality without religion has been ably exposed by Professor Otto Pfleiderer, a non-Catholic thinker of great weight. We will quote a short passage taken from his *Evolution and Theology and Other Essays* (*Essay IX*):

> "Morality stands or falls with the absolute obligatoriness of the consciousness of duty, which renders the general laws and purposes of society binding on the individual, and with the certainty that the ethical end can be attained in the world. Some basis or sanction for the unconditional authority of duty must therefore be found, and this cannot be discovered in the will of the individual, or in that of a number of individuals. Still less can it be derived from that which is lower in the scale of existence than man, namely nature. Natural laws and impulses by no means correspond exactly with those of morality, and indeed must be subordinated to the latter, and given a moral character from them. Hence the moral sanction must have a transcendental ground; it must have as its basis some absolute super-subjective rational will, i.e., God."

The argument may be reduced to this: Why should I be responsible to my fellow-men for my moral actions? Something outside and above a number of individuals, something to which I perceive myself responsible, must demand my allegiance. I have no moral responsibility except to God. No God, no moral responsibility.

And yet, in spite of this fact, which, to those who believe in God, is as plain as the sun in the heavens, Humanitarians rely for the attainment of their Utopia on heroic unselfishness in men, arising from an intense conviction of moral responsibility to their fellows, without any rational basis for such a conviction. Further, even if what Mr. G. A. Smith, in his *Little Essays in Religion*, calls the "religion of Humanism that is gradually but surely superseding the religions of supernaturalism" were to be so strongly impressed upon men that theoretically they accepted it, would the appeal to Humanity present a strong enough motive for heroic unselfishness in actual life? Would the appeal be strong enough to repress in men all those desires which run counter to the worldly good of mankind? Take the case of adultery. Adultery is undoubtedly a bad thing for social life. It is an abominably selfish kind of crime. How would the Humanitarian appeal affect an adulterer in real life? I will imagine, for argument's sake, that I am a Humanitarian. I come across a man running off with someone else's wife. He and the lady are on the point of stepping into a first-class carriage at Paddington Station. I grasp the situation. I advance, raise my hat, and address the gentleman as follows: "Sir, adultery undoubtedly causes much confusion in family life and society. If you give vent to your desire for this lady, grievous harm to posterity may result. You are running counter to the good of mankind in embarking on this course of action. I therefore appeal to you in the name of Humanity to desist." How would the gentleman reply? I am strongly of the opinion that the only response to my appeal would be a forcible slamming of the carriage-door and, possibly, a generous application of adjectives to Humanity.

In real life the appeal to Humanity without God could only have successful results if it openly took the form of an appeal to self-interest. A mere vague appeal to a fanciful Utopia of happiness, to be somehow attained at some time in the future, if men will conform their lives to an even vaguer standard of pseudo-morality, can carry no force with it. Man, prone to evil, needs a powerful deterrent, not milk-and-water sentiment. The appeal to "pure altruism" is more futile still, as we shall prove later.

We see, then, that Humanitarianism can neither propose a satisfactory deterrent from evil nor offer a serious inducement to good. Until it can, Utopia may wait. Religion, on the contrary, offers me a solid rational basis for morality. Religion tells me *why* I should avoid evil and *why* I should do good. Religion tells me that in God alone can I find the principle of moral obligation: that God is the supreme legislator of the moral order. God is my Creator. I am His subject. He has absolute rights over me. God is my First Beginning and my Supreme End. I owe everything to Him, the homage of soul and body. From Him I receive my being, my faculties, my activity; hence I must direct to Him all my aspirations and devote to Him my whole moral life in complete submission to His Will. The realisation of the happiness which I necessarily pursue demands the employment of my entire nature in His service. If I disobey His moral laws, I miss my final end. If I obey them, I win Eternal Life and everlasting happiness. Religion thus gives my moral actions an absolute and eternal value. Humanitarianism gives them no value at all.

Religion treats me as a rational being. Humanitarianism treats me as an unthinking dupe.

CHAPTER VII

Altruism, False and True

WE HAVE GIVEN the reasons for our belief that the Humanitarian appeal to mankind could never carry with it sufficient conviction either to deter men from evil or induce them to lead the moral lives so essential to the establishment of a worldly Utopia. And now, in order to drive home the folly of those who are allowing themselves to be victimised by the loose-thinking prevalent today, we shall investigate the doctrine of *irreligious altruism* so fondly cherished by these devotees of Man.

This doctrine inculcates sacrifice of self for the interests of others, without any religious incentive for the same. We are assured that there is a natural impulse in man towards self-sacrifice. True, but observation proves that this impulse accounts for very few acts of a self-sacrificing nature, and those too of a special class. In the vast majority of cases, when men sacrifice themselves in the interests of others, they do it for an ideal, or for a religious motive, or under the influence of a Christian environment. And therefore, human nature left to itself, as it actually is in the Humanitarian scheme, would be bereft of almost all the conditions requisite for producing self-sacrifice. Ideals would ebb away. The religious motive would be there no longer. As for Christian environment, we need not reckon with its influence as a stimulus to altruism, because in the Godless system under discussion, Christianity would be relegated to the realms of outer darkness. We have to imagine a condition of things in which the thoughts of men are not even coloured by religion; that blissful state around which the supporters of the *Literary Guide* form an imaginary circle and dance for joy. Probably the majority of those, however, who today profess the Humanitarian creed, are still under the influence of emotions which have borrowed their glow from some religious association or other. All unconsciously they are pursuing religious ideals. A small minority, it is true, may be gifted with a temperamental capacity for self-sacrifice. But it is with the mass of men we are concerned, and with whom also the Humanitarians are concerned.

The masses, robbed of religion and religious influence, would tend to selfishness, not self-sacrifice, however urgently it were pressed upon them that the road to general happiness must be paved with the latter virtue. If I were to choose any twelve men and, conceivably, deprive them of all religion and all religious influence, I am morally certain that from that moment worldly self-interest and not self-sacrifice would dominate their actions, in spite of every Humanitarian argument I were to put before them. To quote cases of noble self-sacrifice amongst the heathen is valueless, because the heathen are not deprived of all religion. On the contrary the natural law of God is written in their hearts. Those of them who do live up to ideals are the very ones who are observing the natural law, and therefore living with a certain divine light in their souls.

On what grounds, then, do we believe that, normally, self-sacrifice is very difficult of accomplishment without the stimulus of the religious motive? To sacrifice himself for the sake of others, a man has to enjoy the happiness of others more than his own. He has to be capable of vicarious happiness. Is this possible? Yes, when, under certain conditions, what is gained for others far exceeds in value what is lost by self. Why does a man give his life for another in a shipwreck? Because the life of the other man becomes invested with an immense value compared with which the saver's own life seems to matter little. At the moment under the stress of heroic impulses, he actually prefers the happiness of the other man to his own. In a word, under abnormal conditions, men are capable of acts of heroic self-sacrifice. But, under normal conditions, men, left to themselves, are not capable of acting in this heroic manner; and still less of continually sacrificing themselves. Modern commercial and business life afford ample proof for this. Moreover, in cases like that mentioned, the act of heroism may be due to the man acting on an ideal, which, though he may not know it, is implanted in his heart by his Creator.

In ordinary hum-drum life it will be found that the less religious men are, the more selfish; the more truly religious men are, the more self-sacrificing. The life of continuous self-effacement is the normal thing within the Religious Orders of the Catholic Church. That is why it is possible for thirty men or thirty women to live together in peace. The same number of irreligious men or women cooped together for life would probably be squabbling, if not scratching, at the end of the first week. Outside the Religious Orders self-effacement is found only among the few. In the world, as a general rule, men take a back place in the interests of others or push for their own worldly happiness just in so far as they are more or less religious. Intense unselfishness always attracts attention, thus proving its rarity. The common thing escapes notice. Selfishness is a common thing. Only two men in ten give up their corner-seats in a railway carriage from sheer unselfishness. Five out of ten would do it from shame. Nine out of ten if the lady were attractive. The two do it from a religious motive—for the love of God. They may also do it because of an ideal, i.e., because, unconsciously, they are acting Godwards. The five might not do it at all, if they could decently avoid the shame. The nine do it to obtain the lady's favour, i.e., from a selfish motive. That is, roughly, what happens in all the affairs of ordinary everyday life. Take away religion, and you would have no genuine self-sacrifice left; for ideals would vanish rapidly as well.

Do Humanitarians expect to change human nature radically? Search their system from top to bottom, from end to end, and you will find in it nothing which could change a selfish man into an unselfish one. The futility of their appeal even to keep a man from evil has already been exposed. Much less will that appeal induce men to lead the lives of "pure altruism" needed for the very first stages of the journey to the Promised Land.

Driving pigs to market becomes child's-play before the task of driving Humanity to Utopia. You can compel the pigs to reach the market-place, but you cannot compel men to attain ideals. You cannot compel them into unselfishness. Morison, apparently intending to suggest that somehow or other unselfishness can be compelled, pictures the selfish man, who refuses to sacrifice himself for Humanity, arraigned before an imaginary tribunal of idealists. From the lofty heights of pure altruism they address him in terms of withering scorn: "From you, sir, we expect nothing; but *you* may expect that your shameless confession of selfishness will not go unpunished." That is a typical instance of loose-thinking. How can the man be punished? Given a caning? Hardly. Social ostracism? Impossible; for then the majority of men would have to suffer the same fate. A majority ostracised by a minority would be too ludicrous. Moreover, why should the poor man be punished at all on Humanitarian principles? To Morison and the like-minded all virtues and vices are but inherited instincts: "Their presence or absence in the individual is no merit or fault of his. Nothing is more certain than that no one makes his own character. That is done for him by his parents and ancestors." If these premises were true, why should the selfish man even be ashamed? He cannot be blamed for what is not his fault. Why be annoyed with him? The same petulancy is noticeable in Mr. Wells when inveighing against such traits in human nature as he deems inimical to the advance of his schemes. It is perhaps a subconscious impatience of the impotency of his principles to compel men to sacrifice themselves for the sake of Humanity. The painful truth will, sooner or later, force itself on the Humanitarian mind that the self-sacrificing tendency is so rarely found without religion that, rather than build upon a negligible quantity, it would be almost wiser to pigeon-hole it as an unknown quality.

We see, then, what this doctrine of irreligious altruism is worth. Its propagators are not merely counting their chickens before they are hatched, but counting without the eggs.

And here we have a bone to pick. Morison speaks of "the love and sacrifice even now to be found in the nobler hearts," of acts done for others with no "thought tending to self-advantage" or reward. Now why should he refer to acts of "love" and "sacrifice" as if they were nobler than selfishness and greed, seeing that, in his view, men have no free-will? The acts of beings, who are no more than animated automatic machines, are neither virtuous nor vicious. I might as well extol "the love and sacrifice" of the penny-in-the-slot machine which supplies me a piece of chocolate with no "thought tending to self-advantage."

Further, Morison relies on evolution to produce in the dim future a race of pure altruists. We must confess our complete failure to perceive how Humanitarianism can ensure the future generations inheriting the virtues of love and self-sacrifice from their ancestors. The ancestors will need a little guidance in the matter themselves. We are also left utterly in the dark concerning the means by which mankind is to be scientifically trained in the cultivation of these qualities. The Catholic Church has been training men successfully in acts of love and sacrifice on behalf of others for two thousand years—witness her Religious Orders; but she has succeeded because she has taught them to love others for the love of God. Will Humanitarians succeed with no intelligible motive to offer for such acts? But stay! There is such a thing as giving up in order to gain. The motive of gain is intelligible. A sincere materialist once wrote: ". . . when we strive to make the world a better place to live in, it is really that we ourselves may have a larger measure of happiness." There may be a race of "pure altruists" yet.

Now it is sometimes suggested that it is Christians who are selfish; that, after all, they are only seeking their own eternal happiness; they are good only for the sake of the reward they hope to gain. Those who challenge Christianity on this score think they have revealed the real motive of Christian goodness. On the contrary they have revealed their own ignorance. What is the aim and object of all our endeavour? Is it our own happiness? Our own self-satisfaction? Is that all the Catholic Church can hold before us? Have all her Saints and Martyrs, all her devout millions, lived and died solely for themselves? Does the whole Christian system, when tested, shrivel into a society of pure egoists? A very elementary knowledge of Catholic teaching would suffice to show that the object of our efforts is not our own selfish happiness. Our object is God. Why are we good? For the sake of God. All our actions, as Christians, tend towards God, our supreme end, our Sovereign Good. We love God, not for ourselves, but for Himself; not for our own reward, but for His Glory. This truth is hymned by old and young, lisped from the lips of children:

> "My God, I love Thee, not because
> I hope for Heaven thereby,

.   .   .   .   .

Not with the hope of gaining aught;
Not seeking a reward;

.   .   .   .   .

Solely because Thou art my God,
And my Eternal King."

The end of Christianity is to *love*, not to enjoy. Eternal happiness is the *consequence* of attaining God, and is desired only in its relation to Him. It is true that the average Christian's love for God undergoes a progressive purification. He begins by loving God for his own sake, for the sake of his own happiness. He ends by loving God for God's sake, for what He is. The Christian has then become a pure altruist, because a pure lover. His own interests have been absorbed in the interests of God. We would ask our critics, therefore, to judge us, not by our failure, but by our intention, to love perfectly. Let them also judge of Christianity by what it teaches, not by the frailties of its followers.

There are others too, the "Humanitarian Christians," who look upon Catholics as too much absorbed in the next world. We can but reply: "No, you are too absorbed in this." These well-meaning Modernist-Protestant philanthropists have half an eye on Heaven, but one eye and a half on the earth. They are really putting man's life on earth before his life in Heaven. They are putting man first and God second. As in the twilight objects are distorted, so in the gloom of Modernism Man looms large and God seems small. Ultimately, for those who follow this path, the darkness will blot out the last rays of the glory of God. It will then be all Man and no God. In the Catholic Church, where men live in the full blaze of Heaven's light, they see God's Immensity and the nothingness of man. They put God first and their fellow-men second; and that is why they love them better than those who put them first. To love men for the love of God is better than to love them for the love of themselves. It is a higher way of loving them. It is loving them from a higher motive. And from the only adequate motive.

In the long run men do not love others sufficiently to serve them except from the love of God.

CHAPTER VIII

Men As They Are

I T IS A QUESTION whether, eventually, men *could* love one another at all without the love of God. Listen once more to the sapience of Professor Pfleiderer. We quote from the same *Essay IX*, as before:

> "When love for mankind in general is no longer the result of religious belief, as it is with Christians, but rather a substitute for it, it is a serious question whether human beings as we actually find them are so amiable that we can continue to love them, and devote all our energies to their service. When the philanthropist is rewarded by bitter ingratitude and his noblest endeavours are frustrated by man's dullness and wickedness, will not his courage fail and his enthusiasm be quenched, if he is not inspired by a belief in the Good which transcends this world of appearance."

That piece of wisdom is worth considering. It is pathetic to see a brilliant spokesman for Humanity, like Malcolm Quin, pouring out his prevailing passion on paper, and all to no purpose. This fervent writer has actually produced two large volumes urging the Catholic Church to let go her hold upon the supernatural, and instead, placing herself at the head of the Humanitarian movement, lead men onwards, amidst the acclamations of the world, to the glories of "the Human Republic." How can she deny what she has known from the beginning, that the love of God must come first and the love of man will follow? It is futile to retort: "Why then has the Catholic Church failed to establish the brotherhood of man?" It is not the Catholic Church which has failed, but the world. Men have failed to sacrifice themselves for the love of God: to subordinate their temporal to their eternal interests. They have refused to loosen their hold on the glittering baubles of earth. Once that grip is loosened, self-sacrifice in the interests of others becomes easy. The more fondly men cling to the world, the more fondly they hug its gifts to themselves, the more selfish, the more worldly they become. And that is exactly what Humanitarians want men to be—*worldly*. It is the wildest folly to expect a world concentrated exclusively on itself to breed unselfishness. As well expect a brothel to breed purity! To urge altruism and worldliness in the same breath is like urging a man to walk in two opposite directions at the same time.

In addition to the external difficulties confronting "pure altruism," there is a certain factor to be reckoned with, which will prove an even more formidable barrier to the efforts of those who call for self-sacrifice without religion. That factor they ignore or deny. It is this. There is a *persistent tendency* in human nature to turn to selfishness and vice. The incontrovertible facts of history testify to this painful truth. This evil inclination of the human will is as strong today as in the ages of the past. Were the Humanitarian Eugenists to weed out all the backward, unfavourable, criminal, megalo-maniacal, and vice-ridden types in the world, nevertheless in the select remainder this tendency to selfishness and evil would still crop up. And Humanitarians have no means wherewith to counteract it. Were the most perfect civilisation conceivable achieved, it could but cleanse the surface of human life: underneath corruption would still pursue its course. Men would be merely whited sepulchres. There is surely something wrong with human nature. And as wrong today as ever, in spite of all "progressive evolution." What it is we shall subsequently explain. Human nature, left to itself without religion, is strangely averse to altruism.

That is man as he is. In vain will Humanitarians harp to him the sweet strains of "pure altruism." Deaf ears will be turned to the harping. But sound the loud note of the world and its pleasures, and ears will be deaf no longer. Persuade men to serve Humanity for the sake of their own individual interests, and they will understand and respond. Not a single conscience among them will be bluffed by the doctrine of irreligious altruism. It rings false and will deceive no one. As we read Morison and Wells, it becomes more apparent in every line that this appeal to man's nobility is mere white-wash, unrecognised as such by themselves, maybe. Remove the white-wash, and the summons to Mankind reveals itself as a summons to the individual to secure for himself the maximum of worldly happiness. In the case of Wells, the appeal is largely to man's sensual nature and the gratification of his passions. These worshippers of Man could but turn men into worshippers of themselves. That, and no more. Were it possible for the Kingdom of Man ever to be realised, it would prove to be, not what they picture it, but a kingdom of diabolical selfishness, wherein men would defiantly serve Humanity to secure for themselves the highest possible measure of this world's pleasures.

A veritable Kingdom of Hell on earth.

Chapter IX

Soft Sayings and Hard Facts

A SERIES OF ESSAYS destructive of the Humanitarian theories but unproductive of a solution of the essential problem concerned—the problem of human happiness—would be of little value. We shall, therefore, make it our business to offer the true solution of that problem.

It is to be found in the acceptance of truth. So strangely seductive is the flame of falsity to the ready moths of our modern world, that only a powerful counter-attraction, if any, can lure them from their danger. That counter-attraction is truth. Truth is wondrously alluring to her lovers. The false philosophers, false theorists, and false religionists of today, although the enemies of truth, yet call themselves her lovers. That is why they gain a hearing. In reality they love not the truth, for the truth is not in them. They purr forth soft sayings, for the liking of a soft generation. Stern facts are not for such as these. Truth comes, not softly clothed, but clad in mail. Those who would win her must face facts fearlessly. It is a stern fact we now intend to propound.

We have seen that there is a persistent tendency in man towards selfishness and vice, which will prove a grave obstacle to the progress of Humanitarianism. The fact of this tendency, though it does not actually prove, at least renders agreeable to reason that revealed truth of God which is commonly called the Fall—the Fall of man into sin. This revelation discloses that human nature is not as God originally intended it to be. It has fallen. Human nature created to crown the universe has fallen from its majestic heights into the abyss of sin. It lies weak and wounded, wallowing in the mire. The mire of evil holds it, sucks it down. That revealed truth, at any rate, offers a satisfactory explanation of man's peculiar tendency towards selfishness and sin.

The modern world, of course, blatantly rejects the Catholic doctrine of the Fall into sin. The writer of a recent article in a weekly paper informs us that "The modern science of psychology has no use for the doctrine of original sin. . . ." Possibly not. I have no use for psycho-analysis, as practised by certain quacks; but, for all that, it exists and does untold harm. We are also assured by the enlightened ones of today that "sin" can be explained by the theory of evolution; that man is evolved from the monkey; "sin" is merely the relics of monkey-nature, old monkey-habits breaking out. We cannot help wondering why these modern lights are so desperately anxious to prove us evolved mind and body from the monkeys. Of course, if we are, it relieves us of all responsibility for our moral conduct. We can blame the monkeys for anything we do. A criminal is merely a person with monkey-habits still too strong. A man, for instance, induces his rich aunt to make her will in his favour. He then proceeds to hit aunty on the head with a hammer. It is unfortunate for aunty; but, after all, it cannot be helped. It is merely an old monkey-habit coming out. These monkey-tricks will be evolved out of us in time. We can assure these materialists that they will not.

Man is not evolved from the ape. His body may be: but man is not a body. He is a rational soul and body. A rational soul cannot be evolved from an ape. However, we are not concerned to prove that. A gratuitous assumption is sufficiently met by a gratuitous denial. We should also like to point out that experience of life contradicts the materialist's theory of sin being due to an animal origin. Man is possessed of reason and will. And yet, in defiance of right reason and with full consent of the will, men act contrary to the right ends of animal nature. They pervert animal nature. Witness the drunkard lying helpless on the pavement. Witness the drug-sodden maniac. Witness the lovers of Sodom and Gomorrha. There are men today who practise unnatural vices of the vilest kind. They act as no animals would act. They may be highly civilised, but they are not fit to associate with pigs. This capacity in man for descending below the level of the ape is scarcely compatible with the theory of his ascending from the same. When will these shallow theorists cease from doping the masses with the notion that "sin" is merely the monkey coming out? Why persist in duping the credulous into the belief that evolution and the veneer of civilisation will cure the evil that is in the world? As well expect to cure consumption by putting brilliantine on the hair!

Why is the present-day world fevered with this anxiety to put itself right, without the help of the Almighty? To save itself without asking God to save it? For the simple reason that it refuses to admit itself a fallen world in need of God's help. And so men struggle and muddle along, immersing themselves more deeply in the mire, pretending there is nothing really wrong, crying "progress" when there is no "progress," calling for a new world which ever tarries and does not come, pursuing a fantastic idea of some future Utopia of happiness on earth, fooled by false deceivers who may thank the intellectual decadence of the age for whatever acceptance their tomfooleries may win. There is no hope for the world but in the acceptance of the revealed truths of the Fall and Original sin; for, strangely enough, to accept them is to discover the entrance-gate to human happiness. From that entrance-gate there runs a royal road laid by God, wending its way from earth to Heaven. A way of sorrows passing through a vale of tears; a way of thorns that turn to roses; a way of peace that passes understanding; a way of faith foreseeing the unseen; a way of hope piercing death's dread portals; a way of love losing itself in Love Eternal; a way of unearthly beauty illumined by the dawn-light of eternity; a way of happiness undimmed by any shadow of an ending, entering the Heart of the Everlasting. It is called the way of grace.

But enough of that way now. We must first tell of this world's tragedy—made known to us by God Himself. In the knowledge of this tragedy lies our safety. Believe in the Fall and you will believe in Christianity. Deny it, and you deny Christianity. For if the Fall is but a myth, then the life and teaching and death of Christ are meaningless, we need no Saviour or salvation, the whole of the Christian religion is sheer folly, Christians are a pack of fools, and we may as well consign Christianity to the gutter. The Fall happens to be true, however. God has told us so Himself. God ought to know.

Why not face it?

Chapter X

The World's Tragedy

WHAT HAPPENED at the Fall? To understand what it was we will look at man, first before the Fall, and then after it; at man as God made him, and then at man as he has made himself. And we will look, not from within, but from without; from, say, an angel's point of view.

. . . One day, thousands of years ago, an angel hovered in his course over a garden. It was the Garden of Eden. And in the garden a man and woman were walking. The angel descended into the garden and looked at the man and the woman. They were very beautiful. And the angel looked at the animals in the garden. They were beautiful, too; but not in the same way as the man and the woman. And the angel saw the difference. "God," said the angel, "has breathed on the man and the woman, and made them living souls; and in their souls they are like God." For the angel knew what God was like. He could see God face to face. And the angel perceived that their souls were pure and white, and there was no stain of sin upon them. He knew what sin was like. It was black. He had seen Satan cast down to Hell all blackened with sin. And the angel saw a golden radiance in the souls of the man and the woman that never ceased from shining. "That," said the angel, "is God's gift to them—sanctifying grace. It is the secret of their beauty and holiness. It is the secret of their friendship with God." And he noticed that, though they had passions, yet those passions were under the control of their reason. He noticed how God had enlightened their reason with great knowledge. Nothing hurt or harmed the man and the woman. They had power over all the animals in the garden. No suffering touched them. No shadow of death lay across their pathway. For they ate of the Tree of Life. "Yes," said the angel, "they are very beautiful. There is nothing in the whole world like them." And the angel passed out of the garden and upwards, and gave glory to God.

But, in the garden below, there was another tree, the Tree of the Knowledge of Good and Evil. And in its shadow a dark form stood. Satan was watching the man and the woman.

.   .   .   .   .

One night, thousands of years later, the same angel hovered in his course over a great city. He looked down upon the city, and descended into it. Instead of one man and one woman, there were vast multitudes of men and women. And everywhere were glaring lights and places of amusement, cinemas, theatres, music-halls, night-clubs. People were rushing about feverishly in search of pleasure. Painted women were bargaining with men for the price of their bodies. Newspaper placards boomed the latest sensations, the latest scandals, the latest divorces, swindles, and robberies.

The angel passed down a side street. From out of a drinking saloon came two men. They were drunk and quarrelling about some woman. They lurched down the street hurling filthy abuse at each other. They entered a house together. Inside they grew more violent. One of them drew out a knife and struck at the other. In a frenzy of hatred he stabbed him again and again and cut at his throat, until the other fell down dead. Then he kicked the dead body and spat on it. He went out, locked the door, and staggered away.

The angel came to a large building. It was a chemical-works. Inside one of the rooms a man was working. His head was bent over some glass tubes. He was inventing a new form of poison-gas. And, as he worked, he muttered: "If I can get this right, my fortune is made; it would kill off a whole city."

The angel passed into an open space. A man was addressing a great crowd. He was telling them that men who believed in God were fools. From time to time he broke out into blasphemy. He sneered at religion. Suddenly he held up a crucifix and spat at it.

The angel passed down more streets. He noticed so many evil faces, selfish faces, faces of animals. He noticed how the crowds were absorbed in the pursuit of sin; that the things of the world mattered so much, and the things of God so little.

The angel passed out of the city, and upwards. And he thought of the man and the woman in the Garden of Eden, and then of the men and women in the city he had left. He looked down on the glittering lights below. "Yes," he said, "they have fallen as low as that.". . .

That is a portrayal of man as God made him and of men as they are now; not of men who have risen from their fallen condition, but of those who remain fallen or have fallen back. What happened to man that he should become so changed? Do you remember Satan watching the man and the woman in the Garden? He seduced them from their God. They disobeyed the Divine command. They fell into sin. Into the very sin that Humanitarians would see perpetuated—the sin of preferring themselves to God, of preferring the creature to the Creator. Do you remember how beautiful the man and the woman were who walked in the Garden? Do you remember the wondrous gifts with which God had endowed them—the supernatural state of sanctifying grace, knowledge, control of the passions, freedom from suffering and death, dominion over the animals?

They lost all those gifts when they fell into sin. They were stripped of their glorious garments. Their beauty was marred. The image and likeness of God was blurred. And all that they lost, we have lost too. They represented the human race, and the human race fell with them. Their sin is inherited by their descendants. It is a family inheritance. It is called Original Sin. That is the world's tragedy. The human race is a fallen race.

You say: "But, it's not just that I and the whole human race should inherit the sin of Adam. It's cruel that the sin of one man should result in the downfall of all men." One minute. Are you quite clear as to what Original Sin is? It is neither personal sin, nor actual sin. It is a sin of nature, a *birth-stain* upon our human nature. You and I did not inherit the personal, actual sin of Adam, but the stain of it. And are you quite clear as to what Original Sin consists in? It consists in this—that we enter this world deprived of sanctifying grace and of those other gifts with which God endowed Adam and Eve before their fall. You say: "Why should not I have a right to those endowments?" I answer: "Because they are all God's *free gifts*." We have no *right* to the free gifts of God. Also they were bestowed upon the human race on condition that its head remained faithful. Adam was not faithful. Moreover, God has deprived us of nothing which belongs to our human nature as such, for instance our natural faculties. We have not been deprived of our rights. We have lost privileges which might have been ours.

Again, God does not leave us in our fallen state, although, if we choose to remain in it we can. God has placed the Catholic Church in this world to help men escape from their fallen condition. By her means He will wash men white and clean from the stain of Original Sin in the laver of regeneration. At the touch of her hands sanctifying grace is restored, and lo, once more we become the friends of our Creator, His children by grace, and heirs of Eternal Life. Thus does the Catholic

Church minister to men in dire need on earth. And, through her lips, there comes the solemn promise of God that those other gifts, though lost awhile, shall yet be ours again—that the beauty of the man and the woman who once walked in the Garden shall one day be perfectly restored to us in Heaven.

You say: "If the stain is thus removed and sanctifying grace restored, why do so many of the cleansed and sanctified fall back again? Why do even those who are advanced in the way of grace still feel the terrible attraction of sin?" I answer: "Because human nature has been shaken by its fall." A man who has fallen from a height is so shaken that the effects of the fall may last for life. It is the same with us. Until the end of life on earth, our human nature feels the effects of the Fall. It has been wounded. It is out of control. It suffers from a kind of mental blindness whereby sin seems so attractive. It suffers from a weakened will whereby it tends towards evil. This tendency is diminished to vanishing point when grace has raised a man to heights of sanctity. It has full play in those who remain fallen, those who have never taken the hand of God held out to raise them from the morass.

Those are the plain facts about man which Humanitarians would do well to face. They are painful facts. Accept them, and the key to the problem of human happiness is found. Deny them, and the way of release is closed and all hope gone. It is cruel bluff to tell men that they are not fallen; for if men do not believe it, they will never seek the only way of escape from their fallen state—the way of Redemption, the way to happiness untold. We have no hesitation in saying that Humanity's worst enemies are those who pose as its best friends, the Humanitarians themselves. Not only would they close the road to human happiness by their denial of revealed truth, but they open wide a road to ruin in its stead. At its entrance they plant a sign-post—"To Utopia." It should read—"Abandon hope, all you who enter here." For those who take that road their last state shall be worse than their first. It is the open road to Hell.

The suicidal folly of denying the Fall is now apparent. We willingly admit that there is much relating to it which we cannot understand; but let no man for that reason "lift his daring to the stars" and defy the Almighty for further explanations. It is not ours to question, but submit. There are those who think it a sign of intelligence to deny the revealed truths they cannot fully understand. They are the fools. The supreme folly is to make our own reason the standard of truth. The supreme wisdom is to recognise that our minds are finite, and that God is Infinite. When God speaks, let men keep silence. It is the fool who jabbers on with his everlasting "why?" If the "Rationalists" would but reason, they might discover that the highest rational act lies in accepting the limitations of the finite mind. As for demanding an explanation from Him by Whom we live and breathe, upon Whose will we hang as a stone upon a string; surely it does not require a very profound insight to perceive that the Creator is under no obligation to explain to His creatures.

Can we not rest content to understand in Eternity what is hidden in Time? And, if ever we feel baffled by the great mystery of the Fall of man, or, if ever we are tempted to murmur at God for allowing such a tragedy to take place as the downfall of our human nature, then, lest we question Infinite Love, let the remembrance of an even mightier mystery prevail and stem tempestuous doubts:—

It was the same Eternal God of love, Who, looking down in pity on us, came down from His throne in Heaven, took our human nature upon Himself, and was made Man. And, as Man, He suffered under the Fall, not as we suffer, but immeasurably more, and in agony unspeakable. The curse of Adam rested on the sinless Son of God.

And He never murmured.

Chapter XI

The Humanitarian Challenge and an Answer

Lest enthusiasts for social reform should deem these essays to be unappreciative of the same, we would hasten to assure them of their mistake. We have ignored the question of social reform, not to belittle the efforts of sincere philanthropists, but to fix attention on the problem of human happiness, which, in itself, is quite independent of social conditions. Our arguments are directed against the Humanitarian scheme for the world's reformation and salvation.

That scheme is inimical to human happiness. It omits deliberately God and religion. Whether the world could put itself right without God, as far as material prosperity is concerned, is open to question. It might be allowed to do so for a time. But a state of society resultant from such irreligious efforts, however prosperous, would not be happy. A monstrous business concern for the sharing of profits would be achieved, no more. An Utopia of calculated self-interest. Men serving Man for the sake of themselves. The great God, Humanity, might find men prostrate beneath his pedestal; but the homage offered would be that of greedy time-servers. Though stocked with earthly goods the Kingdom of Man would yet be empty of the *unum necessarium*. The world would not be really right. The world could never save itself. Its salvation does not lie in material prosperity at all. There is only one salvation that matters for this world, and that is salvation from sin. Sin, as a matter of fact, is the root-cause of almost all social evils. Humanitarians think otherwise. "How enormously," says Mr. William Archer (*Literary Guide*), "would the political problems of Europe be simplified if the idea of sin . . . could by some miracle be eliminated from the minds of the various populations!" On the contrary, Mr. Archer may congratulate himself on the fact that the political problems of Europe have been enormously complicated *by* the elimination of the idea of sin. To ignore this is merely to put one's head in the sand. We should have thought that the notion of sin was conspicuously absent from the minds of men today.

The world is shelving the unpleasant idea. Even Modernist "Christians" are putting sin in the background. Social reform seems of more importance than salvation from sin. That is why Christ is looked upon, outside the Catholic Church, as a mere social reformer instead of a Saviour. The Sermon on the Mount is patronised. Calvary is ignored. Calvary reminds us of sin. The world is only interested in the Cross to the extent of inviting Christ to descend from it: "Come down from the Cross, and we will believe in you! Come and reform social life. Come and settle between Capital and Labour. Come and stop war. We will accept you as a social reformer, but not as a Saviour. We are not interested in the Cross and salvation from sin." That is a fairly accurate voicing of what the world asks of Christ today, if it asks anything of Him at all. His crucifixion and all that it stands for barely interest the mass of men. There is a certain public holiday which was once a public Holy Day. It is called Good Friday. That public holiday in England has become a public insult to Christ crucified. The pathos of all this folly is enough to make the angels weep. As if the world could be put right by social reform! As if the world could be put right without men being put right! As if men could be put right without God!

What is God's way of putting men right? God's way is to put men right with Himself. God's way is called—the Redemption.

When the human race fell into sin, an injury was done to God. An insult was offered by the creature to his Creator. An infinite wrong—because the Infinite Majesty of God was offended. And an infinite satisfaction had to be made to God, before men could once more be put right with their Creator. Who was to make this infinite satisfaction? No mere finite man could. It needed an Infinite Being to make the infinite satisfaction. And only God is Infinite. What did God do? He became Man. He who knows human nature in all the nakedness of its sins yet found it so lovable as to assume it Himself. God the Son took our human nature upon Himself. He became "bone of our bone" and "flesh of our flesh." He became one with us. Why? To restore our human nature by sharing it with us; to undo the tragedy of the Fall; to represent the human race to His Father; to offer the infinite satisfaction for the wrong done. The God-Man, Jesus Christ, took our human nature and united it to His Divine Nature. He placed the hand of man in the hand of God. He linked together Heaven and earth. And only the God-Man could do that. How was the infinite satisfaction rendered? How were we put right with God? How did the God-Man redeem us? He died for us a bloody death. The Precious Blood was the price paid. He gave His life, as He Himself declared, a ransom for us. His Father had so willed it. He obeyed.

That is the Catholic doctrine of the Redemption put in the very simplest form. And it is against the Redemption that Humanitarians and Rationalists thunder their special indictment. On their own principles, of course, they must necessarily object to a doctrine which enshrines the Divinity of Christ. The objection, however, as actually formulated, is grounded upon their own twisted notion of the method employed by God to redeem mankind. Will these good people never take the trouble to read a little Catholic Theology? Why insist on presenting perversions of Christian doctrines? Why endeavour to make out that the idea of the Redemption is brutal and repellent? Listen to Morison: "The notion that God wanted to be propitiated by the death of the innocent Christ is a thoroughly base and barbarous one; . . . Hardly the most depraved man, in his right mind, would accept the vicarious punishment of one who had not offended him in lieu of one who had. . . . Yet this cruel and barbarous notion is the centre of the Christian religion; . . ." Notice the implication that Christ was brutally dealt with, as if His own will in the matter were not taken into account. This *argumentum ad populum* is an excellent specimen of the methods employed against Christian doctrines. The charge might be justified had God the Father forced His Son against His will to die for us. Do those who pour such contempt on the idea of the Redemption imagine such to be the case? Their argument is shattered by the simple fact that it was equally the will of God the Son to die for us. He did it of His own free-will, gladly, lovingly: "I lay down My life for My sheep. . . . I lay it down of Myself," declared the Son of God. "And I have power to lay it down; and I have power to take it up again." It was a free-will offering. The voluntary offering of the Precious Blood is of the very essence of the Sacrifice of the Cross. Moreover, since the Son of God is God Himself, His will is one with His Father's. The Son, Whose human body died on the Cross, *is* God. The foolish cavilling of our opponents is equivalent to charging God with brutality to Himself. No, the Redemption does not reveal cruelty or barbarity. It reveals love. God must love His human creatures with a love that passes understanding to give His only-begotten Son to die for love of them.

The Redemption is God's answer to those who challenge His love.

We would note, *en passant*, the despicable attitude adopted by many at the present moment who challenge the love of God. Encouraged by the Positivist and Humanitarian teaching of half a century, the world succeeds in ousting God and His revealed truths from its midst. The only adequate bond of brotherhood, the love of God, is broken. Then, instead of acknowledging the horrors of the European War to be the consequence of its own act, the world accuses Christianity of failure and defies the Almighty to defend His reputation for love. A gang of school boys, listening to evil counsels, refuse to acknowledge their master's authority and teaching. Disrespectful to the master, they become disrespectful to one another. Squabbling ensues. Then, instead of acknowledging the trouble to be the consequence of their own act, they turn on the rest of the school, accuse it of failure, and defy the master to defend his reputation. That gang of school boys would be treated with scorn by all fair-minded people. Their attitude would be considered despicable. We leave the moral to be drawn.

To return. Why is the world challenging the love of God, challenging His goodness, challenging His supposed silence and indifference to evil and suffering, challenging His very existence? The Redemption has been forgotten or denied. That is why. Of course there are evil and pain and suffering in this world. There *is* the problem of evil. There *is* the mystery of suffering. Do Christians deny it? We neither deny it, nor do we deny God because of it. And, at least, we do admit sin, the only evil, strictly speaking, to be *our* failure, not God's. And we do know that God is not silent to His lovers. For the rest, we are content to wait a while without understanding. Do "Atheists" solve the problem of pain and suffering by denying God? They merely place themselves and their dupes in a worse position than before. To sulk at the Infinite God because He has not chosen to reveal how these things are worked into His eternal purpose is hardly a rational proceeding. The Catholic Church answers the world's challenge by proclaiming the Redemption. She reminds us that the God Who created this world, in which there is evil and suffering, is the very same God Who redeemed it by sharing that burden in person. She silences the derisive taunt—"Where is now thy God?" by pointing to Christ agonising and dying on the Cross; "Here, here in the very heart of the world's evil and pain, here is our God!"

Yes, Christ hangs there on the Cross.

And that is the one thing that matters. Did the European War matter compared with that? Do politics matter? Does scientific progress matter? It is the Crucified Who matters. The eternal destiny of every living soul hangs on that pale, blood-stained Figure.

Yes, He hangs there.

And there are thousands to whom it means nothing. It means nothing to them that their God hangs on the Cross. That is why a pagan cenotaph, and not a crucifix, stands in the middle of Whitehall.

Yes, He hangs there.

And all the while men are conscious of some great burden resting on this world. They feel it pressing them down. They seem almost unable to perceive what it is. It is the same burden that rested on the God-Man in Gethsemane. The burden of sin. The burden which He bore to Calvary. There is only one way in which men can be released from that burden—by taking their sins to Calvary. It is humiliating, of course, to come and kneel beneath the Cross.

But it is more humiliating to hang there.

Chapter XII

Human Happiness

WE NOW APPROACH the problem which, above all, occupies the world's attention at the present time— the problem which Humanitarians hope to solve, but cannot—the problem of human happiness. Its solution is quite simple—divinely simple. To accept the doctrines of the Fall and the Redemption is to find the entrance-gate to human happiness. We will explain.

The Redemption, which is Eternal Love countering the Fall, alone gives entrance to the *way of grace*. That way is the way of happiness, the way of eternal life. It leads into a *supernatural* world. Many today assume a blank air when "grace" and the "supernatural world" are mentioned. Some vaguely imagine that the "supernatural" is what Theosophists and Christian Scientists and Spiritists deal with; whereas these pseudo-mystics in reality are dealing either with the psychical or with humbug. The supernatural world, or the world of grace, is an Inner Kingdom. A Kingdom, not of this world, but from above. A Kingdom of living, quivering, intense reality. A Kingdom within which God admits those who respond to the Redemption. Admittance is gained by co-operation with the Redeemer; by the acceptance and reception of the grace won back on the Cross—the grace lost through the Fall.

What is *grace*? It is the life-power of those souls within the Kingdom. A gift of God—a special creation—unseen, but utterly real. Nothing in the order of nature can produce it. Only God can create it. It is a *super*-natural help given by God to our souls. With it we can work out our salvation. Without it we are as helpless as a bird without wings. Grace is the gift of gifts from God to men, because it saves men, not only from the effects of original sin, but of all actual sin. And the way of grace is the Kingdom's highway. By grace, and grace alone, we enter into friendship with God, the friendship forfeited through the Fall. By grace we become His children. By grace we become the heirs of Heaven. By grace we enter Heaven. By grace we see and possess God eternally in Heaven. By grace we attain unending happiness. The unutterable value of the gift of grace won back upon the Cross is now apparent. A beggar in rags who possesses grace is immeasurably greater than a king without it: for the beggar is within God's Kingdom; the king is outside. As Eternity is above time, as God is above His creatures, so is grace above all the things of this world. In this supernatural Kingdom of grace alone is to be found that perfect happiness which God intends for His human creatures.

This Kingdom is none other than the Catholic Church of Christ—not as a visible body, but as an invisible realm. Even as God Himself is not seen with the outward eye, so also is His innermost mystery of grace veiled from the rude gaze of the world. And the Kingdom, though not of this world, is yet within it. The walls and gates and ramparts can be seen, but not that which is inside. The inner realm of grace is for those alone who enter. The hidden treasure is within. Humanitarians may pour their scorn upon the Catholic Church, but they are perpetually baffled by her peculiar hold on the souls of men. Her secret is hidden. A holy secret. Are pearls to be cast before swine, or that which is holy given to the dogs? The mysteries of God are hidden from the wise and prudent and revealed to the babes and sucklings. It is the humble of heart who enter and understand and learn the power of grace. And millions and millions of fallen men have proved for themselves, and are proving for themselves today, that the Catholic Church can and does lift them right out of the mire in which they are struggling. She bids them in the Name of Jesus Christ arise. And they do arise. She gives them God's grace to do so. She leads them to the Crucified. She wields the power of the Cross. She has the power to apply to the souls of men the graces of Redemption. From the Cross there flow seven streams, seven streams of life, seven streams of grace—the seven Sacraments of the Catholic Church. She can wash the robes of men and make them white in the Blood of the Lamb. She, and she alone, is commissioned by the Crucified to do so. Every single sin-laden man or woman has but to come to the Catholic Church and cry to her: "Let me in, set me free from the dominion of Satan, give me life!" And the gates of the Kingdom are opened and she sets them free and gives them life—the Life of their Saviour and Redeemer.

It is only left to us to indicate the nature of that perfect human happiness found within the Kingdom of God's grace. When we say "found," we do not mean that those who enter the Kingdom instantly attain to perfect happiness. A journey lies before them. The King's highway passes through this vale of tears. The way of grace is, at its outset, the Way of the Cross. The sanctified are privileged to share with the Crucified. But suffering so shared is haloed with divine light, and sorrow turned to joy. From Calvary the soul first sights Eternity—and God. And in the bliss of this preliminary experience all earthly pomps and pleasures and promised Utopias fade away into petty insignificance. Gone is the glamour of the world at the first glimpse of its Creator. Creation pales before the Uncreated. The human soul set free from sin and graced perceives what the world blindly ignores—the Object of all desires, the Source of all happiness—God Himself.

With unerring instinct the sanctified soul "senses" God as its final end and supreme happiness. Even at the early stages of the way of grace there is vouchsafed a foretaste of That which alone can satisfy all the aspirations of human nature—the Infinite. The finite can never satisfy the soul of man. Humanitarians think otherwise. The whole of their Utopian edifice is erected on the erroneous supposition that human happiness can be attained here on earth. It cannot, and it never will be. All the things of the world and all their vanishing glory could never satisfy one single human being; a truth the world seems almost incapable of appreciating. One by one life's trumperies are grasped by greedy hands. One by one they turn to ashes. One by one each long-sought treasure fails to satisfy. "Lo here, lo there is happiness," men cry, and clutch and clasp. But in the very clasp it's gone; and men are left—still craving!

No created thing can constitute man's happiness. The object capable of providing happiness must satisfy all desires and must endure. In no created things are these conditions verified. Their insufficiency to satisfy is due to a deficiency of intrinsic quality. Wealth, honour, renown, power, bodily health, beauty, sensual pleasure—all that men count so dear—not only are these perishable, but of a lower order than man himself. The goods of life are imperfect, as lacking the whole perfection of which man is capable and for which his being yearns. Man tends naturally towards something higher than himself— towards the Perfect Good. This tendency is implanted in the innermost recesses of his nature. That Perfect Good can alone fulfil all his aspirations and desires: therein rational beings can find their rest. To possess that Perfect Good is to possess Perfect Happiness. The Perfect Good has no ending. It is God. And God is Eternal Happiness.

Thus does perfect happiness await the pilgrims of the way of grace. God Himself is the solution of the problem of human happiness.

.   .   .   .   .

Our task is now accomplished. We have endeavoured to delineate as accurately as possible the two ways which lie before humanity today. As far as can be judged, the majority of people in England, unseeing the fateful issues, are hesitating as to their choice. Protestantism has been tried and found wanting. It is being quietly deserted. Humanitarianism and Catholicism, which is Christianity, remain. The Christian way looks hard and rough, yet leads to happiness. The Humanitarian way looks smooth and alluring, yet leads to disaster—to the greatest disaster that can befall a human being—the everlasting loss of Eternal Happiness—of God. Those who choose this latter way and make this world their end are cutting themselves off from the end for which they were created. And their choice will be final. There can be no undoing of this life's choice. The consequences are eternal. Every man can choose or refuse the Divinely appointed way to happiness. Every man fixes his eternal destiny for himself. Every man, who wishes, can find happiness in God's way. No man can find it in the Humanitarian way.

Of what avail, then, the defiant boastings of Humanity's braggadocios, their puny pretences, and high-sounding sophistries? Humanitarians may sneer at the Christian "myth," undermine the weak of faith, succeed in hoaxing thousands. What then? Let men "laugh at the things they had feared" and "lift their daring to the stars"; let the "Great Revolution that is afoot on Earth" capture the very world itself; let the Kingdom of Man be proclaimed and the Kingdom of God cast aside! What then? Let Eugenists breed the finest and fittest—Gods and Goddesses; let free-love reign supreme; let science eliminate all that is painful and distressing! What then? *Fiat Regnum Hominis! Fiat* Utopia! *Fiat* a world of "men like Gods"! What then? What gained? What won? A glut of all this world can give—no more. What lost? The one thing sought—the happiness of man. And with it all is lost. That Kingdom too will vanish, Gods, Goddesses, and all; sink to the nethermost depths of Hell. They flouted God, flung back His love, denied His truth. They made their choice and fixed their fate—eternal banishment.

So shall men end who make themselves "like Gods."

.   .   .   .   .

In the dim ages of the past God said: "Let us make man to our image and likeness." Thereby He crowned creation. Thereby He raised man above all created things of earth. Thereby man's soul was created a spirit to be *like God*. By grace the likeness is perfected:—

There, in eternal realms beyond, divinely dignified,
Illumined with God's glory, God's Nature shared by grace,
Pervaded through and through by Love, and Holiness and Truth,
The finite face the Infinite, men see God face to face:
Partaking God's own happiness, transfigured, deified—
Not to become that which God is, but sons, co-heirs with Christ,
Sharing the Royal Sovereignty, crowned with the crown of Life:
So shall men end *whom God makes gods* to the image of Himself.

THE SHADOW ON THE EARTH

A Tale of Tragedy and Triumph

PROBLEMS OF HUMAN HAPPINESS. II.

NOTE

THIS present volume is the second of a series. Though complete in itself, it deals with only one aspect of a very big matter—the problem of human happiness. It should be read in conjunction with *Will Men Be Like Gods?* the first of the series, which it follows.

May I mention that I am fully aware of the sensational character of much that I have related here. I make no apology for the same. It is unavoidable. I am dealing with a terrific thing. I am dealing with life as it is.

The problem of pain and suffering, with which this book is concerned, is prominent in the minds of men today. Unfortunately many only know it as presented by life's rebels—coloured with malice, twisted with cunning sophisms. It would seem to be the delight of certain writers to dangle the problem on the point of a vitriolic pen and hurl it at the heavens in defiance. These rebels offer no solution of the problem of pain and suffering. Instead, they sound the clarion of revolt.

They have no solution to offer.

There *is* a solution, however. It is offered in these pages.

AUTHOR.

CONTENTS

THE SHADOW ON THE EARTH

CHAPTER I

Broken

IT WAS A MONASTERY on the lower slopes of the Alps. It was night. And it was a knocking on the outer door loud enough for the great awakening that roused the monks from their slumbers. One of them went down and opened it. Outside three men were standing, bearing a roughly-made stretcher on which a dark form lay.

"There's been an accident on the mountains," said one of the men. "May we bring him in?"

The monk led the way to the guest-room. The unconscious figure was laid on the bed.

"I will go and fetch Brother Anselm," said the monk, adding that Brother Anselm used to practise as a doctor. He left them. They stood staring gloomily towards the bed. One of them muttered his annoyance at finding the place was a monastery.

A few minutes, and Brother Anselm entered—an Englishman to their surprise. He looked at the three men—rather sharply at one of them; then went across to the bed. They explained how it had happened. He got to work and examined the battered body. He set a broken limb and bandaged some cuts. Next, leaving a monk in charge, he found food for the other three. Beds were prepared. No, said Brother Anselm, he would watch; they needed sleep. As he kept vigil he recalled the face of one of those three men—the face of a man he had once known.

In the morning he examined his patient again. And then he gave his verdict.

"Yes, he will live; but he will be crippled for life. The spine is injured."

A second doctor was sent for from the town down in the valley. He gave the same verdict, adding that there might be a good deal of pain from time to time.

．　　　．　　　．　　　．　　　．

The day came when the sick man asked Brother Anselm how soon he would get up. When would his legs be right?

Brother Anselm did not answer, but looked at him. He was thinking how young he was. His physique was splendid, his good looks unquestionable. The features, the way of the hair, the shape of the hands told of breeding. There was something very attractive about him, too, as he had already found.

"When shall I get up?"

"Would you rather I answered your question quite straight?" said the monk.

"Why—er—yes, of course."

"You will never get up."

The other stared.

"*Never get up?* What—what do you mean?"

"You will be a cripple for life. Your spine is injured."

There was a silence—a horrible silence. The young man turned white. He lay there thinking.

"Is that true?"

"Yes, it is true."

The meaning of it slowly came to him. The monk saw a gleam entering his eyes, and his fists clenching. The bed suddenly shook. . . .

"Curse it! . . . Curse God! . . ."

Brother Anselm did not stir.

"Yes—curse God! . . ."

Brother Anselm waited.

"I hate Him! He's smashed me up!" He choked it out, his voice shaking.

"God did not smash you up," said the monk.

"Oh, don't put me off!" The other glared at him. "Why didn't He stop that blasted rope breaking? Why didn't He stop me from falling?"

"Why didn't He work a miracle? That's what you're asking."

"All right, then. Why didn't He?"

"Why should He? Is He under any obligation to work a miracle?"

"Yes, if He's any good. What's He for, if He's not for that?"

"He's not for interfering with His own laws, without good reason. After all, you take your own risk on the mountains."

"His laws have done for me, damn them!"

"You are not done for," said Brother Anselm.

"*Not done for?* I'm broken! I'm finished! My life's finished; everything's finished—finished. Do you hear? Do you understand? It's the end of everything."

"It is not."

"Not? Don't try and blind me. I—I don't want your apologies for the Almighty. I don't want your religious talk: you needn't try it on me. I've done with religion. I never had much use for it. I've none at all now."

Brother Anselm waited, saying nothing.

"Don't stare at me! Can't you say something? Can't you do something? You people can't do anything when your religion's put to the test. Why don't you get your Almighty to put me right——"

He stopped. His ear had caught something. It was the monks singing their Office.

"Go and tell them to stop that row! Tell them to stop that fool's game! And, if He doesn't put me right, tell them to curse Him!"

Brother Anselm took up a book and began to read.

The other subsided into a sullen silence—broken by occasional mutterings. He began to think. He began to think deliberately, fiercely. He thought of all that life had meant to him; of his undergraduate days, of his games, his triumphs, of the cups standing on his mantelpiece at home. He saw them standing there now—in mockery. He saw the colours of the county he played for, hanging in his cupboard. His mind travelled to the stables: he was patting the silky neck of his favourite mount; swinging himself into the saddle. Then to the garage—his car. He was on the road—switching her on to the full; trees and hedges whistling by. Then his friends—his endless friends, bridge friends, tennis friends; those summer days on the courts—tea inside. He could hear the great Georgian house, his home, ringing with their laughter. He saw the sunny lawns in front sloping down to the cool of the trees and river. He was swimming in the clear depths, diving into them off the bank, shouting to the others stripping there, shouting for sheer joy of life.

Great nights in London flashed before him. The Pullman journeys up with that hunting crowd after the day's meet. Dinners, wild dinners—pelting one another with paper balls; mad pranks—men and women well champagned, flushed with the day's wind and drink. Afterwards the show—annoying the sedate stalls with their tomfooleries. Or the Savoy—the sensuous rhythm of the jazz band. Faces came back to him—faces of the women he had danced with, fooled with; faces of the women he had loved. Then Prince's for supper—and a night-of-it. . . .

Yes, that was life; gorgeous, full-blooded life! . . .

Suddenly he came back to realities—to what had happened. The horror of it returned—redoubled. Sweat broke out on his forehead. He tried to shift himself. Brother Anselm looked up to see him glaring in impotent frenzy.

"It's the end of everything! I'm in a trap! It's a living death! I'll go mad! . . . I'm not going to lie here. I'm going to get up——"

He struggled to rise, wriggling towards the edge of the bed. Brother Anselm went across quickly and held him down.

"Take your hands off!"

"I will not."

"Take them off!"

"I will not."

He lay there gasping.

"I will let go when you give me your word to lie quiet."

"You damned bully!"

"You may damn me as much as you like. Are you going to keep quiet?"

He yielded angrily.

"All right, you brute of a monk, I'll give in; but I'll not forget this."

Brother Anselm let go. He went back to his chair and picked up his book again. The other lay still; his lips trembling, his eyes closed.

Half an hour later he fell asleep, exhausted.

CHAPTER II

The Cripple and the Atheist

§ 1

"**N**OW THAT you're here," said the Cripple, "I want to talk things out. I'm in the depths of depression. You realize my position, don't you? I am done in. There's nothing to look forward to, but lying on my back like a helpless log for the rest of my life. Cheerful prospect, isn't it?"

The Atheist sat down by the bed. He had climbed up from the hotel in the town at the foot of the mountains, where the three of them had been staying since the night on which they had carried their burden into the monastery. He was the eldest of the party: the one whose face had recalled some memory to Brother Anselm. It was certainly a face that would not be forgotten easily. Its singularity lay not so much in the straight features, startlingly handsome though they were, or in the blackness of the eyes, but in the peculiar, cynical twist of the mouth. It was a clever face, revealing a powerful personality behind.

"I am sorry," he replied. He passed a hand over his hair.

The Cripple began to tell him what the monk had said on the previous day: Brother Anselm had talked quietly to him later on. He was calmer now and could speak collectedly. The Atheist listened. The cynical twist of his mouth became more marked.

"Oh yes," he said as the other came to an end, "but I am afraid this good monk's arguments sound somewhat unconvincing. These religious people have got to say all that. It's their profession—their job. Did his apologies for the Almighty convince *you?*"

"I scarcely listened. I didn't want that kind of stuff. It bores me stiff."

"I'm not surprised. Apologies of this nature are apt to be wearisome, and forced." There was a wariness in the tone, as if he were feeling his way. He crossed his legs.

"These people, you know, call their God a God of love." His manner was indifferent.

"So I believe," said the Cripple, equally indifferent. The Atheist went further:

"Can you seriously imagine a God of love creating a world like this—a world whose pains and horrors give the lie to anything suggesting love?"

The Cripple looked interested.

"I can't say I've ever thought much about it. Go on."

The Atheist moved forward his chair:

"Can you believe in a God Who is eternally silent to the cries of tortured humanity? Can you believe in a God Who looks down upon the world in cold aloofness, Who never shows Himself, Who never makes a sign? Can you really believe in a *good* God creating men and breaking them on the wheel of life—as He has broken you? If there were a day of judgement, it would be for man to appear at the bar not as a criminal, but as an accuser. If I were ever to believe that a God of love created this world, from that moment I should consider myself insane."

The Cripple was roused now.

"What sort of God created it, then?"

"We've no reason to suppose it was created at all. It's always been going on."

"But how? Something must make it go on."

"Certainly; some sort of eternal energy—a blind force."

The Cripple pondered, staring at the wall opposite.

"Well," he said at last, "supposing there is no God; supposing I'm the victim of a blind force instead of a God; I don't see that I'm any better off than before. It doesn't put me right. It doesn't help me. Can't you see? I'm caught—pinned down! I can't escape! Oh hell! Can't you see, man?"

The Atheist hesitated. . . .

"You mean you want something to live for?"

"Y—es; if you can give me something."

"Listen. Live for Humanity. Put the idea of God away. The day is coming when men will no longer cringe before a God in a distant heaven and a future life: that idea has had its run. It is Man now—Humanity! Let Humanity be your God. The future is not in another world: it is here. There is a dazzling future ahead—on earth. Science, genius, all the powers of human reason are even now uniting in the only cause that matters, the future of mankind. Soon the whole world will be dominated by one sentiment, one idea—the reign of Man. Man, no longer crushed, but conquering; chaining the very forces of nature, casting out disease, riding down rough-shod all that is hideous and ugly. There is a heaven coming. It will be man's own creation: it will be this world transformed. The future lies with Man, not God."

"But I shan't be there," came testily from the other.

"No, but the memory of you will be—of your share in bringing it about."

"My share!" A bitter laugh broke from the Cripple. "Can you see me transforming the world on my back?"

"The world will be transformed by the spread of reason, the steady progress of reason; by the rooting up of false ideas, of mediæval superstitions; by teaching men to rely on themselves and not on an imaginary God, to concentrate solely on this world, on this life, not on an illusory future invented by priests—in a word, by spreading truth. Why not study the works of reason? You have a clear intellect; why not use it? You will have leisure. Even on your back you will have abundant opportunity of influencing others. Combat these false ideas. Why not further the cause of Humanity by——"

"Oh, hang Humanity! Excuse me being rude, but I haven't the slightest interest in it, or its future. Humanity can get on without my luminous intellect to enlighten it. Intellect? I'm not fool enough to be taken in by sop like that. Even if I could do what you suggest, even if I did share in bringing about this wonderful future, what good would it be to me? I shouldn't be there to enjoy it."

"You and your work would live on in your fellow-men," said the Atheist.

"And I am to spend my future non-existence in oblivion of that consolation? How very comforting! Thank you, but I am afraid the prospects of Humanity don't appeal to me on those terms."

The Cripple thought. Then he said:

"I don't wish to seem ungrateful, but—er, may I be quite candid?"

"Certainly. I'd rather you were. Remember, I have merely suggested *one* course."

"Well then. You give me, if possible, even less to live for than before. If there were a God and a future life there would be something to hang on to. You say there is not: you take *that* from me. You know too—forgive me being quite plain—you know quite well that, in your rationalistic scheme of things, I could never be anything but a burden to others—to Humanity. I am helpless, smashed up—useless. I am one of those *ugly* things you mentioned that ought to be got rid of; scrapped, thrown into the dust-bin. You know quite well that I—and all life's miscarriages—are on your list marked 'unfit for further use.'"

"Rather a bald way of putting it; but still if you feel——" The Atheist purposely left the sentence unfinished. The Cripple regarded him curiously for a moment, before he continued:

"You once spoke to me of your utilitarian ideas—eugenics for the human race: the unfit were to be weeded out; the old, the sickly and the *crippled* were to be offered, politely offered, euthanasia. It should be gently but firmly impressed upon them that they were clogging the activities of their fellow-beings, that they were in the way. I remember the very illustration you gave—a marching army hampered by its wounded. Life, you said, was essentially the vanquishing of the weak. The unfit must drop out, Humanity march on. And I agreed with you then, when—when I was wanted. I am one of your unwanted now——"

"And do you agree now?" cut in the Atheist. He had shown no sign of embarrassment. He was watching the Cripple intently.

"I don't know." The Cripple paused. "I don't know——" He looked up, to be met by a cold, calm stare. Suddenly a fury seized him, and for a moment he saw red. . . . He held himself in. Then he said deliberately and calculatingly:

"I don't know. But there is one thing I *do* know. I asked you for something to live for. You offer me—you don't say so, but it is what your ideas mean—you offer me the choice of burdening the world with my broken body or of getting out of the way. You offer me death for preference; and after death extinction. You take away everything and you give—nothing. I asked you for something to live for: you offer me nothing—to die for."

The Atheist looked out of the window.

.   .   .   .   .

§ 2

There was an odd look in the Cripple's eyes. He had lain there very still, after the Atheist's footsteps had echoed his departure down the corridors of the quiet monastery, and died away. The evening had faded slowly into night, into the vast blue canopy stretched above the Alpine heights. There was silence in the night. There was silence in the heights, silence in the valleys, silence in the monastery, silence in his room.

A bell pealed into the deeps of it all—and into the Cripple's brain. He stirred uneasily, and then became aware of things—of the door opening. Brother Anselm stood before him. He felt himself being raised. A cup of something was placed on the bed-table. He began to drink, mechanically. Brother Anselm seemed to be watching him.

"Don't stand there looking at me!" he snapped out. Brother Anselm sat down and began to say his Office. When, later, he was removing the empty cup, he said:

"You've something on your mind; won't you tell me?"

The attempt was greeted with a laugh—a bitter, sneering laugh. The Cripple lay still again, staring unseeingly at the wall.

"Good night," said Brother Anselm. The Cripple took no notice. There was a puff at each of the candles and then darkness. . . . Suddenly he became alert. He listened. He heard the door shutting. He waited. . . .

Then slowly, painfully, he shifted his body to the side of the bed. His hand felt downwards, underneath. The knapsack was there. He tugged at it. It was on the bed, his fingers feeling for the straps. He tore at the canvas and plunged a hand inside. Yes, the case was there. He wrenched it out; the knapsack fell with a thud. There was a little button. . . .

The lid was open. His fingers ran over the row of phials. It was the shortest one, he remembered—the one the chemist had warned him of. That—that was it! He drew it out and held it up. Yes, that was it. He could see it silhouetted against the open window. . . . The moments went by. He was still holding the little phial—eyes staring into the blue silence without. Would it be more silent than that? Was the Atheist right? Would it be just—a blank? Suddenly he felt afraid, horribly afraid. The terror of that nothingness gripped his whole being, and set the pulses drumming in his temples. The little bottle slipped from his fingers—now wet and shaking. He clutched wildly and recovered it.

Then slowly his will reasserted itself. He lay still. . . . The little silhouette appeared again—and fingers feeling for the cork. . . .

There was a swift movement somewhere in the room. Something—a hand—was gripping his wrist! He felt his fingers being unloosed, in a steady deliberate way that suffered no resistance. The bottle was released.

He fell back, stupid and dazed. There were more movements in the darkness. A match grated and flared. The candle-flame hesitated, grew, and revealed—Brother Anselm!

It was some ten minutes later. The Cripple was calmer; but the twitching of his lips betrayed the strain of the recent crisis. Brother Anselm had not spoken. He had merely flung the phial out of the window, picked up the knapsack, put the case inside, and then sat down and resumed saying his Office. . . .

"How did you know?"

The monk looked up.

"I saw it in your eyes."

There was another pause.

"How did you get in?"

"I never went out."

"You—you were here all the time?"

"I was."

Brother Anselm laid his breviary on the table. "There are only three people who know what happened just now; you and I—and God. It is known only to those three. You understand?"

"Y—es," said the Cripple, and then he added: "Thank you."

Brother Anselm did not pick up his breviary again. He looked at the clock on the mantelpiece and then sat rather intent as if waiting for something. It came. Through the open window there floated, rising and swelling and sinking, the strong cadence of the monks' Office: *De profundis clamavi ad te ...*

"Do you know what that means?"

The Cripple shook his head. Somehow he could not speak.

"From the depths I have cried to Thee."

The Cripple looked away, rather queerly, as if not wanting to be seen. His lips tightened—and quivered. A spasm shook him—a jerking, difficult spasm of sobs. And then the floodgates of his soul gave way, and down the pallid cheeks there streamed an agony of tears. . . .

Brother Anselm was by the bed now, his hands on the pathetic heaving shoulders, a world of pity in his voice:

"Oh, my man . . . my poor man . . . my poor man. . . ."

Chapter III

The Monastery Garden

IT WAS a week later.

The doctor had come up again from the town below and re-examined the Cripple. He and Brother Anselm had then held a consultation. It was decided that the patient might now be moved.

Brother Anselm was telling him. The Cripple, however, did not seem enthused with the idea.

"I was wondering," he said rather wistfully, "if I might be allowed to stay on for a bit."

"There would be no difficulty as far as *we* are concerned," replied Brother Anselm. "It is you I am considering. Don't you think you might be rather bored? We are a bit religious here, you know. Of course, if you feel you can stick it——"

"Can you stick *me*?"

A big brown hand was held out. The Cripple took it shyly, eagerly:

"I want to stay, if—if I'm not a burden."

Something in the answering grip told him that he would not be a burden here—not one of the unwanted. Brother Anselm stood looking at him for a moment and then turned away, and for no apparent reason began to examine the book-shelf. . . . He was blinking.

And so it came about that the Cripple stayed on.

It was now full summer. The icy wind from the Alps no

longer whistled and screamed under the eaves of the monastery roof. Instead, the sun poured down invitingly. Through his window the Cripple could see the snows of the mountains glistening white to its blaze.

One day there arrived a kind of long chair on wheels—an ambulance. Next day the Cripple was lying in it, in the monastery garden. And there, from now onwards, it became his custom to spend the long summer hours.

It was very beautiful in the garden. Flowers of gorgeous colours and scents patterned great carpets of green. There were trees too, in clumps, for the wind's whisperings. From their shade he could see the grassy slopes giving way to fields, and the fields to the grey of the rocky valley, and, far away, the hazy plains of Italy. On either side there towered the great white Alps.

It was here one morning that Brother Anselm sat, reading to him. A gorgeous morning. Insects droned and buzzed in the quivering heat all round; the tune of some near-by stream tinkled its way over pebbles and rocks; there were birds on the wing and their songs in the sun. There was peace.

Brother Anselm became aware that he had lost his audience. He stopped reading. It brought the other back from his reverie.

"Sorry. I'm awfully rude. I was thinking about something."

Brother Anselm put down the book, and turned towards him. He noticed there was a difference in the Cripple's appearance. He was no longer unkempt. He was shaved, and his hair was glistening and brushed well back. These matters had been neglected at first. His good looks were very apparent again.

"Er—may I talk to you about something?"

"Fire away."

The Cripple considered how to make a start.

"Well, first. You must have thought me an awful cad——"

"Cut it, man, cut it."

"No, but really——"

"That's all over. Next please."

"I say, it's beastly good of you to——"

"Shut up. Get on with it."

The Cripple gave up.

"Well—er, this is what I want to say. I've been having a sort of think—thinking things out; and I'm beginning to see that it's no good despairing and going mad. It seemed at first as if it was the end of everything. I suppose it is in one sense. I mean that other life, that hectic life, is over—finished. I still feel muddled and confused—uprooted. Things seemed so cruel, so horribly cruel——"

"I know," said Brother Anselm, "I know."

"——And yet life *can't* be altogether cruel. All this isn't cruel"—he indicated the garden—"it's amazingly beautiful. You're not cruel, you're——" The Cripple swallowed. "I mean there's a lot of goodness and beauty in the world: that's what I'm beginning to see. But why—this is what I *can't* see—why should there be so much ugliness, so much pain and suffering mixed up with it all? It seems one huge contradiction."

Brother Anselm gazed at the Alpine snows as if seeking an inspiration. He stood up and moved the Cripple's ambulance away from the green arbour until the whole mountain-range lay bare before them, ridge upon ridge sweeping up into vast white stretches, steepling into peaks against the blue of heaven. He pointed:

"You see those dark patches of rock? They bring out the whiteness of the snow, don't they? They add to the beauty of the mountains. Don't you think, in the same way, that the ugly patches in the world, the dark patches of pain and suffering, might bring out the goodness of life—might add to its beauty?"

The Cripple studied the mountains.

"Y—es, I see. Y—es."

"Is what has happened to you really an unmitigated disaster?" said the monk. "Is it really a cruel horror? Why shouldn't it add to your life, in some way? It has cut you off from a great deal, yes, including that hectic life, as you call it; from animal pleasures, from the inane futilities—the silly shams of a world that dares not think, that jazzes along on its brainless round of shows and drinks and lusts: a lunatic's 'Dance of Death.' It has cut you off from all that. And it has left a void. Don't you think that possibly that void may be a good thing?"

"How? Why?"

"Because voids can be filled."

Brother Anselm wheeled the ambulance back into the shade. The Cripple did not say anything. His eyes were still upon the mountains. . . .

"You tried to escape from life. You ran amok—went off the deep end, because you thought there was nothing left."

"You mean there is something more, something to fill the void? How am I to fill it?"

"That depends on yourself."

The Cripple saw that Brother Anselm meant it to be left at that. He returned to his former point:

"Tell me, why should there be ugly things at all? Why *should* there be pain and suffering? It's all such a mystery. Couldn't things have been—managed better? Couldn't—— Hullo! who——"

Brother Anselm looked up. A figure was coming towards them.

"It's 'The Optimist'!" said the Cripple.

CHAPTER IV

Brother Anselm and the Optimist

§ 1

H E CAME STRIDING across the grass—and a flower-bed—
to where they were sitting in the shade. Brother Anselm knew him—the younger of the three who had
carried the Cripple down to the monastery on that tragic night.
"The Optimist" was the Cripple's name for him.

"How are we? How are we?" this person exuberated in vibrant tones. "What air! What——"

"It's all right," said the Cripple to Brother Anselm. "He's
pumping up. It's a habit."

The Optimist was taking in deep breaths, signifying the
same with alternate undulations of the chest and abdominal
regions.

"Do stop those pneumatics! We are discussing big things.
You'd better join in." This from the Cripple again.

The exuberant one, having attained the right air-pres-
sure, spread himself on the grass and surveyed the other
two with an all-embracing smile. He was the embodiment
of life and vigour, of physical energy—bristled with it from
head to foot.

Brother Anselm had already found him an interesting
person, with very strong views on life, very pugnacious over
them and very anxious to air them. There had been one or two
friendly scraps between them before now. Untrammelled by

what he called "the outworn dogmas of religion," his intellectual activities found play in such pastimes as Christian Science. The doctrines of Nietzsche shared his attentions. Also H. G. Wells. And he Couéed daily; at cock-crow, morn and eventide. Snippets and tags culled from his heroes' somewhat divergent philosophies of life, and repeated at intervals, supplied fuel for the fervid aspirations of his soul. What he aspired to Brother Anselm could not quite make out. He called it "the realization of the divinity within," but became vague when asked to explain. As a reward for Nietzschean proclivities the Cripple had labelled him "The Magnificent Blond Beast." And he rather looked it sprawling there on the grass.

"You were talking. What's the argument?" he beamed at them.

"Put that last question again," said Brother Anselm to the Cripple.

"Why is there pain and suffering in the world? That's what I was asking," he replied.

The Optimist sprang like a terrier on a rat: "Suffering? Pain? No such things! Inventions! Illusions!"

"Don't bark," said the Cripple. "I knew you'd say that. Er— is this trouble of mine an illusion?"

"Ah, that's because you don't understand. If you understood the Divine Metaphysics of Christian Science you would realize that there is no such thing as matter. There is only Mind. The——"

"Excuse me interrupting," said Brother Anselm, "but, instead of Mrs. Eddy's generalizations, wouldn't it be better to answer the question? Is his accident and all the pain of it merely an illusion?"

"'There is no pain in Truth, and no truth in pain.'" Mrs. Eddy's dictum came out pat. "As long as you think wrongly, you will think as you do about it. It's a matter of right thinking."

"I should have thought it was a matter of fact," answered the monk. "Suffering and pain are self-evident facts, unless we're all lunatics. Is it 'right thinking' to sweep aside the age-long experience of mankind, to deny what is confirmed by universal consent? If Christian Science is true, then the human race is a race of imbeciles. Right thinking? If Christian Science were right, human reason could never be trusted again. Who is Mrs. Eddy to turn up in the nineteenth century A.D. with no credentials beyond a presumptuous claim to a special revelation and a marked ability for writing jargon? Who is she to pit herself against the common sense of humanity?"

The onslaught was unexpected. The Optimist steadied himself with more "pneumatics," seeking for a suitable tag.

"Pop-guns out of action! Get your heavies on him!" encouraged the Cripple.

The tag would not come. The text-books did not provide for this. Finally he tried to manœuvre the corner with: "Don't forget there are thousands of Christian Scientists."

"Yes," said Brother Anselm. "And why? Because there are thousands for whom Christian Science provides a nice easy platform for sliding off from Christianity into paganism, and because there are thousands who won't have pain and suffering."

The Optimist saw an opening: "And you insist on pain and suffering, you Catholics; and in doing so you land yourselves in a very nice dilemma. If there are these physical evils, then there are defects in the world. I'd very much like to know how the infinitely perfect God you claim could create a world with defects in it?"

"That's a heavy," muttered the Cripple. He was all ears now. This was his own question, in another form.

"God could create any world He chose," the monk smiled back, "with or without defects. If He couldn't He wouldn't be God. God can do anything He chooses. You can't limit the

Creator to a particular creation. God is infinite—unlimited. Actually He has created a world *with* defects in it; but these defects do *not* argue against His infinite perfection."

"What? A God of goodness and a world of pain?"

"Certainly. There is no contradiction. Pain and suffering are defects, permitted by God, yes; but defects in a relative sense only—I mean relative to physical well-being. They are not strictly evils, but the natural accompaniment of sentient life. Why shouldn't God create beings liable to pain and suffering—provided, of course, that His eternal purposes are served by doing so?"

"Oh, I don't know anything about 'His eternal purposes.'" The Optimist sounded impatient.

"Exactly. And therefore you are scarcely in a position to judge. If the end of man's creation were merely material comfort and prosperity, then I admit it would be extremely difficult to reconcile pain with perfect goodness. The humanitarian world of today places its chief good in material well-being and is up against God because pain and suffering are in its way— the folly of the thwarted child that sulks. But supposing pain and suffering minister to man's great end; supposing by their very means that end is most perfectly realized—supposing that to be so—then the goodness of God is not in question."

"The great end!" exclaimed the Optimist, ignoring Brother Anselm. He stood up and walked about. His eyes were shining. "The great end! Yes! To attain it pain and suffering must be despised—laughed at, denied! The very notion of them is fatal to man's end. Real or unreal, I would shout from the house-tops: 'Down with pain! Down with disease! Trample them under! Cast them out! Barnacles on the bark of humanity!' How can they minister to the great end of man? The end? Man's end is Superman——"

"Keep off the flower-bed!" from the Cripple.

"——Efficiency! The will-to-power! Defiance! Those are the ministers to man's end. Disease, weakness, pain, these things—I mean these illusions—hang round man's neck like a curse. The unfit—I mean those who think they are—must sacrifice themselves to the earth that one day it may bring forth Supermen. Damaged goods are an encumbrance to humanity. I've no use for Christianity and its sympathy with these horrors—imaginary horrors. It counteracts the law of natural selection—the survival of the fittest. It preserves instead of weeding-out. It hinders, shackles man's whole being, as men will come to see. Man will march on, over the strewn wreckage of dogmas and creeds, to the grandeur of his godhood, to the realization of the divinity within, to the perfect expression of eternal consciousness, to the perfection of himself—which is God! Yes, to his godhood! The earth for the gods—the gods that shall be! . . ."

The outburst was dramatic, but apparently sincere.

"High Velocity!" from the ambulance.

Brother Anselm turned to the Cripple: "Were you with the gunners in the War?"

"I was, yes."

The monk picked a blade of grass and began to suck it.

§ 2

A sense of annoyance pervaded the Optimist, marring the triumph of the moment. Brother Anselm seemed unaffected by the peroration; not even impressed. He suddenly felt young. There was an embarrassing wait. The monk went on sucking the blade of grass. . . .

"Well?" from the Optimist—distinctly piqued.

"Well what?" from Brother Anselm.

"What!—yes, what?"

The monk laughed, but quite good-naturedly. "I'm trying a delay-fuse," he said. "I want you to calm down and listen. May I first remark that the last part of your utterance means nothing to me. And it means nothing to *you*—the 'godhood' and 'divinity' part. These flamboyant expressions mean nothing even to the humanitarians who coin them. They mean no more than the 'Goodness, Beauty and Truth' of the Modernists. It is all so much verbiage, camouflaging the denial of a Personal God and blinding men to their final end——"

"You're evading me," interrupted the other.

"I am not. I'm doing a preliminary canter to clear the ground. Do let's understand what we're talking about. When I speak of man's end, I mean his final end in God his Creator, in Heaven; not an imaginary end in himself here on earth, as pictured by you. That in a moment though. May I make another remark on what you said?"

"By all means." Coldly polite.

"Very well. In your 'gods' and 'supermen' I seem to recognize snatches of Nietzsche and H. G. Wells. I fancy your dislike of Christianity is borrowed too. I am going to be appallingly rude—but have you ever thought out what you have just said? No, you have not. There is no thought behind it. It is quite easy, as many prove today, to rattle off the crude notions of impertinent critics who imagine they can run this world very much better than its Creator. . . . Do you mind sitting down?—Thank you. . . . The humanitarian scheme sounds magnificent on paper, or in the air. In real life this weeding out of the unfit would mean a ceaseless campaign of murder—in Wellsian language 'a certain deliberate elimination'—until a few magnificent monsters were left, devils of selfishness, ruthless unpitying beasts. And they, in their time, might well turn and rend each other, cursing their impotence to find immunity from disease. No. On humanity's brow is written large—'Disease and suffering and pain.' Shall man delete that writing?"

The Optimist was experiencing a sense of deflation. He ejected: "But—but——" and stuck.

"Forgive me if I've been too straight," said Brother Anselm. "Now, here's my real contribution. Granted man's final end as intended by God—that means seeing and possessing God in heaven, and in consequence enjoying eternal happiness, happiness beyond all human imagination—granting that, then a very different light is thrown on pain and suffering. We then see them as constant reminders that man's final aim and happiness lie beyond this world, that he must suffer and endure, that he may not snatch the victory unearned. We see them as rungs in the ladder of life for the scaling of heroic heights. We see this world as a vast crucible into which men are plunged for their testing—for Eternal Life. For those who shirk the test the world becomes a cauldron; for those who face it—a crucible of Love."

Brother Anselm leant over the Cripple:

"Do you understand?"

The pale face lit:

"Yes, the crucible! I—I like that."

"Now," said Brother Anselm to the Optimist, "I want two minutes' private conversation, strictly private, with this—perambulator. I've got something to tell him. Do you think you could sort of run about the garden?"

The Optimist said most certainly he would "take exercise," and walked off, head in the air. Really, this monk was insufferable! Was he a schoolboy?—Damn the flower-bed!—He must collect his thoughts. All that religious stuff, a fool could answer it. Two minutes' private conversation! Bah! Two minutes to put him off! He paced up and down at a distance. . . . Yes, infernally rude of the monk—jabbering away there as if he didn't exist.

That chap Inge was right—a Roman priest could never be a gentleman. More pacing. . . . Two minutes! Twenty more like! Still more pacing. . . . Suddenly there was a crash, and the next moment he was hopping about on one leg. He had failed to notice a garden-barrow left on the path. His expletives were interrupted by a shout from the Cripple: "Don't worry, old man, don't worry! It's only an illusion!"

The Optimist looked daggers . . . and then burst out laughing. His ill-humour had gone.

"Come here," called the Cripple. "I want to say something to you."

The Optimist limped back, somewhat puzzled.

"First," said the Cripple, "put your hand there."

He did so, wondering what this was about.

"Brother Anselm has just been telling me."

"Telling you what?"

"It was you who climbed down and got me up—that night on the mountains."

The Optimist coloured like a boy.

"And you never told me," said the Cripple.

The other stuttered something about it being the sort of thing any fellow would do.

"Not everybody," said Brother Anselm. "Yes, I've found out all about it. You let yourself down into that crevasse; and you knew you might never get back, even by yourself—let alone with the weight of his body. You knew that well enough, and yet you did it. And you only got him back after a struggle that must have been a long hell of torture."

"Put it there again," said the Cripple. The Optimist did so. "You're a brick. You're——"

"That's all right."

The Cripple stammered and became hopelessly mixed— and the Optimist more embarrassed.

"I—I shouldn't be here, if you hadn't done it."

"Damned glad I did it then."

The Optimist was getting redder still. Brother Anselm relieved matters by leading him away. He looked him in the eyes: "I want to thank you myself, for giving me a very dear person to look after."

The Optimist could only blurt out: "It's—it's awfully decent of you to be so gen—generous. Sorry I was so beastly rude just now about your—religion."

"And I'm sorry if I was hard on you. But it wasn't really you I was being hard on: it was those lies—those devil's lies that fool men off the track. I was hard on them because of my respect for you; because I don't want to see a man, like the man you are, being gulled——"

"Look here, you two," interjected the Cripple, "I've got a question to ask. Sit down, Magnificence, and answer this."

Magnificence obeyed.

"May I annoy you?"

"Rather!" replied the Optimist.

"Then tell me. If you really believe, as you said, that the unfit must go, why in the name of Heaven did you save me? You must have known something even then, when you looked down—when you saw my body on that ledge: you must have known that, even if you got me up alive, you would only be salving a bit of wreckage. If you really believe all you said just now, you ought to have left me there—damaged goods, an encumbrance to humanity. You did *not* leave me there. . . . Why?"

There was no answer.

Brother Anselm looked at the Optimist. The Optimist looked at the grass. A bird hopped up, put its head on one side, and hopped off. Brother Anselm looked at the Cripple. The Cripple looked at Brother Anselm. Then they both looked at the Optimist—licking his lips. A clock in the monastery tower wheezed, struck, and saved the situation. The Optimist murmured something about getting back to the hotel. Brother Anselm stood up. . . .

"But——" the Cripple began.

"No, don't," the monk stopped him.

The Optimist looked gratefully at Brother Anselm.

Five minutes later he was swinging his way across the fields. "Good sort that monk," he muttered. "If ever I meet that chap Inge. . . ."

CHAPTER V

A Cry From the Depths

"I CAN'T SEE that it would do him much good: it would only remind him of things."

This was the Optimist's opinion. The three of them were discussing the Cripple in a corner of the lounge. The Atheist had suggested bringing him down from the monastery to spend a few days at the hotel.

"It would be a change," he argued. "It's very slow for him up at the monastery."

"He seemed cheerful enough yesterday: you'd hardly think he'd been smashed up."

The third man—"The Pessimist," as the Cripple called him—growled something about it not making much difference either way: things were about as bad as they could be in any case. . . .

In the end the Atheist prevailed. He seemed quite determined. He would pay all expenses himself.

Later in the day the Cripple received a note, sent up from the hotel. He recognized the Atheist's handwriting, opened and read it through, and then gave it to Brother Anselm.

"What do you think?"

The monk scanned the contents, folded it slowly and returned it.

"There would be no difficulty about getting you down there in the car, as he suggests; and it would certainly be a change. All the same, I don't think you would be any the happier for it."

"Why? Where's the harm?"

"There's no harm in staying at the hotel. I don't mean that."

"What do you mean then? Why don't you like the idea?" There was rather an impatient note in his voice.

"I'd rather not say. I must leave it to you to guess. I'd sooner you decided for yourself, too."

The Cripple considered for a moment and then said: "Oh well, a few days! I can't very well go to the bow-wows now. I'll risk it." He laughed: the scheme was rather attractive.

The car arrived at the monastery the following afternoon. The stretcher part of the ambulance, with the Cripple on it, was lifted in by one of the monks and "The Pessimist," who had promised to superintend the transference—"the transit of Venus" the Cripple called it, excited as a boy off for the holidays. As they drove off he called "Cheerio!" to Brother Anselm, who stood there watching until a bend in the road hid the car from sight.

The monk walked back slowly, wondering whether it had been wise to let him go so easily. He could not prevent him of course. And after all he was not sure. . . . But why was that man so bent on having him at the hotel? Why had that near thing happened on the night of his visit to the monastery—the thing that had so nearly ended it all? Once more certain memories of the past dinned in his brain. . . . Was that man still doing his devil's work? He felt uneasy.

.   .   .   .   .

It was the Optimist. Brother Anselm, looking up from his digging, recognized the swinging stride. He left his spade standing against the wall and went to meet him. Almost before the monk had taken his hand the other was saying—"I hope you won't think me a fool; but I'm a bit worried. I don't like—what's going on down there. It's not doing him any good. That's why I've come up."

"Tell me," said the monk.

The other jerked out his account. It was what the Atheist was doing that troubled him. Brother Anselm's face grew grave as he listened.

"You may tell your friend——"

"He's not really my friend," said the Optimist. "He came with us because he's good at mountains, that's all."

"You may tell your *acquaintance* that, unless he sends him back to the monastery within three hours from now, I shall be down at the hotel an hour later to fetch him back myself."

Within the scheduled time the car was at the monastery gates.

It was Brother Anselm himself now who helped lift the Cripple back on to the ambulance—after taking a note handed him by the driver. The car drove off and he wheeled a silent figure back through the grounds into the garden, asking another monk on the way to bring tea for two. Ensconced in the arbour Brother Anselm opened the note. It contained two lines and was signed by the Atheist.

"*Sir—your 'request' is granted. Our mutual friend has benefited by the change—as you will doubtless discover.*"

Brother Anselm tore the note carefully into small pieces and dropped them on a heap of weeds. Tea arrived. The Cripple consumed it disinterestedly—saying nothing. He had not spoken yet. The monk decided to wait, and busied himself about the garden.

"I wish to hell you'd stop messing about with that rake," suddenly came from the arbour. "I might be a darned corpse for all the attention I get."

Brother Anselm went on with his work.

"Getting me back to this hole——"

Brother Anselm walked across the lawn. . . .

"As regards your first remark—would you kindly keep a civil tongue in your head. As regards the second—you are quite free to return to the hotel. Would you like me to send for the car? I think perhaps I had better." And he went off towards the monastery. . . .

"No, stop! I——"

Brother Anselm walked on. . . .

"No, do stop! I——"

Brother Anselm walked on. . . .

"Oh, I'm sorry—I'm awfully sorry—I'm a cad."

Brother Anselm turned round and came back.

"Will you forgive me? I am very sorry. I didn't mean it. I'm in hell again. . . . Oh, keep me here! For pity's sake keep me here! I've only you—or despair."

The monk sat down close to the Cripple. Yes, those few days had done their work. He set himself to battle for that soul again.

"Tell me all about it."

The whole miserable story came out. The Atheist had looked after the Cripple himself: everything in the way of comfort and ease was supplied. He was kindness itself; insisted on the Cripple seeing the life of the hotel to the full. He would wheel him to the tennis-courts in the afternoon. There was dancing in the ball-room every evening. The Cripple's ambulance would be placed in an alcove so that he could lie there listening to the seductive strains of the music, watching the couples glide by. At first it was rather diverting. He almost enjoyed it; until one night some girl's remark caught his ear—"Poor devil! I'd prefer a coffin—to that."

The words went home like a knife.

"Oh, he must have meant it all kindly; but it drove me mad. I was out of it all—cut off from everything."

"I know, I know, dear man," said Brother Anselm; "but it wasn't only that. You were beginning to face the loss of what you called 'that hectic life.' There was more. Tell me."

The Cripple hesitated.

"There was more, yes; but—oh, I hope you won't think me—disloyal. I told him all you had said—the crucible and all that. He sort of made me. He's got a way of making you tell him things. And then he reasoned. He went on and on, two or three days of it, until the crucible idea looked silly. He said it was one more method of apologising for what he calls 'the ever-absent God.' It all seemed so convincing—horribly convincing. And—and everything went—God and all. He left——"

"He left you, as he left you the evening he came here—in despair," Brother Anselm completed the sentence. "Man, can't you see? He sent you back again today, in despair. He didn't mind sending you back; his work was done—so he thought."

"His work? What work?"

"The work of robbing you of God. Do you imagine he got you down there to give you a good time? He got you there to destroy the hope that was growing in you. You were beginning to turn towards God. He hates God; hates religion. His one passion in life, his one satisfaction, is to rob men of both. That is his life-work."

"But how—how do you know?"

Brother Anselm's reply did not come very readily.

"Because this is not the first time that man and I have met. Last time was years ago, and under very different circumstances. He has forgotten me. I would rather not say more, except that I have not forgotten him."

The Cripple was puzzled, but did not press him further.

"Now," said the monk, "I want you to answer me. Were you happy that day here in the garden when I spoke about the crucible, and God?"

"Yes, I was."

"Why?"

"Because—well, I felt that if I plunged into the crucible, I mean, if I took what has happened to me in your way, I should find God. The very thought of it seemed to make me happy."

"That's number one," said Brother Anselm. "Now, number two. Were you happy when that man had finished with you?"

"No, I was in utter, hopeless misery."

"Why?" The monk leant forward. "Think, man, think!"

The Cripple met his eyes.

"Because—well, I felt as if I'd lost——"

There was a pause.

"Oh——"

The light of a great understanding dawned:

"Oh, my God! I want you . . . I want you. . . ."

CHAPTER VI

The Village in the Mountains

IT WAS Brother Anselm's idea.

He proposed it at breakfast, the Cripple munching toast. He was due at a village up in the mountains that afternoon. Would the other like to come, too? There was a view he wanted him to see. There was something else he wanted him to see as well. He would send for a car.

The Cripple said he was "all on." He looked amazingly happy, after the crisis of the previous day. At night, when the monk had lifted him into bed, he had ventured rather shyly:

"I suppose I ought to start saying some prayers. I haven't done it since I was a kid. What exactly does one do?"

"Talk to God in your own way."

"But I'm such a rotten blackguard."

"Tell Him that for a start," Brother Anselm had replied.

They set off soon after the midday meal, the stretcher part of the ambulance, with the Cripple inside, and the rest of it on the back of the car. "Looks like a travelling circus," he observed.

The road wound its way up and up through the rocky passes, the car climbing slowly—Brother Anselm's order; the Cripple was not to be jolted. From his stretcher he watched the pageantry of nature passing by, strangely and newly alive to the beauty of it all; great phalanxes of pines patching the road with shadows of purple grey; sudden vistas through the clefts of giant cliffs. Or the way would open out into a basin in the mountains, meadowed and radiant with Alpine flowers of every hue smiling their thanks to the sun that brought them forth. Here, too, the oxen grazed, white and sleek and solemn-eyed, ringing with the music of their bells—that sound of sounds, the haunting melody of the mountains.

They mounted steadily, the air growing keener every mile, and at length the village was gained. It was the highest on the Italian side of the Alps. The car drove up to the entrance of a caffè. The Cripple was again placed on his ambulance, and Brother Anselm straightway proceeded to wheel him off down the street.

"What's this? Sort of trot round?"

"You wait," said the monk.

The Cripple noticed a church ahead and people standing about. The children among them saw Brother Anselm coming, waved and rushed to meet him. They kissed his hand reverently one by one and then, clinging to his habit and trotting alongside, began buzzing questions all together. Who was the signore? Why was he in bed like that? Was he *Inglese*?

Brother Anselm told them—and why he lay like that. The Cripple knew enough Italian to follow some of what was said. The rest he guessed; for a hush had fallen on the children. One little girl ventured to his side and studied him—big-eyed and open-mouthed. She announced that he had "beautiful fair hair" and told him her name was Innocente. Then she stroked his hand with her own little brown one and asked him when he would get better. . . .

"Would you like to be inside the church while I am giving Benediction?" Brother Anselm saved him.

"Rather!" said the Cripple, wondering what "Benediction" was.

They were in front of the church now. A man, a rough peasant, came forward hat in hand from the greeting crowd. Would the *Prete* let him take charge? It appeared that he was the father of Innocente. He wheeled the ambulance through the open door inside and stationed the Cripple at the back facing the altar. Brother Anselm departed to the sacristy.

The Cripple looked about, in a state of amazement. The whole village was here, the great church filled from end to end; men, women and children all silent on their knees, or sitting meditatively. Dogs lay about, curled up in content. One, a late-comer, proceeded to establish itself beneath the ambulance. There was a baby close by, rolling about on the floor in an endeavour to stand on its head. An unsuccessful effort landed it by one of his wheels. The baby gurgled with glee at the find, clutched at the spokes and began a new series of acrobatics. At the altar two small boys in red were lighting endless candles, the twinkling flames shedding a golden glory down the nave.

Benediction began. The Cripple watched. That must be Brother Anselm, the priest far off at the altar. He was wearing some curious clothes. He was placing something high up amongst the candles. . . . The peasants sang. How they sang! The sonorous chant swung and swayed up and down, on and on. They seemed to be all looking at the candles. Was it the candles? No, they were looking at what Brother Anselm had placed there. He wondered what it was.

What *could* it be? It was as if they were looking at *somebody*: there was love burning in their eyes. . . .

Suddenly his intuition told him that God was present to these people!

"The ever-absent God"—the Atheist's sneer came back. Absent? But He was here. He was with them. The very way they knelt told him that; their very attitude, their intense awareness.

They couldn't be like that with a God Who was absent. This was Someone they knew to be intimately present, Someone they were talking to.

A bell sounded. There was a hush. They were all bowing their heads. Brother Anselm had turned round—holding Something in his hands. . . . The Cripple remembered that he was a "rotten blackguard." Brother Anselm had said—— Yes, he would do so. . . .

It was quite a procession that trooped back with the ambulance to the caffè. A tiny boy, all braces and breeches, insisted on pulling in front. The little girl, Innocente, secured the Cripple's hand.

"Cut you out this time!" he called back at Brother Anselm.

Revenge came swiftly. The monk whispered something in the little girl's ear. She hesitated coyly for a moment, finger in mouth. The ambulance stopped. Then she stood on tip-toe and gave the Cripple—a resounding kiss on the cheek!

"When you two have finished billing and cooing," said Brother Anselm to the blushing victim, "we're going to have coffee-and-cakes."

Addios were waved, and the ambulance passed into the caffè garden.

Chapter VII

Brother Anselm and the Pessimist

§ 1

"WHEW!" gasped the Cripple.

Brother Anselm had wheeled him to the garden terrace behind the caffè, a grassy plateau fronted by a low stone parapet over which they were now peering down into the depths beneath. The wall of rock, on which they were literally perched in mid-air, ran down some thousand feet sheer into a black gulf of pine-tops. Over their needle-points birds wheeled in dizzy circles. Beyond and below again the grey-green stretches emerging from the dark of the pinery ran down and down, sloping away to the far-off plains of Italy. Here and there the eye could pick out the white thread of the winding road. Flanking the expanses of the valley and soaring up into the white of their snows the Alpine monsters stood—cold and calm and strong, mighty sentinels keeping guard of the plains below.

And over all the blue of heaven swelled, and slowly swooped, and melted in the distant haze.

The Cripple gazed upon the vastness of it all.

The arrival of coffee and cakes broke the spell. One of the little tables which stood about was placed at his side. Brother Anselm did host and poured out the coffee.

"Shall we ask your friend to join us?"

"What friend?" said the Cripple.

Brother Anselm pointed with his coffee cup to a melancholy figure sitting at the other end of the terrace. The Cripple looked and recognized—the Pessimist!

"Good gracious!" he exclaimed. "So it is! He's come up here to be miserable. Yes, let's ask him. But he's not exactly cheerful, you know. He's got extraordinary views, too."

Brother Anselm went across, exchanged the usual courtesies, and returned with the Pessimist, who was evincing mild surprise at their presence.

"I've just been apologizing for you," said the Cripple. The Pessimist attempted a smile. He was wondering whether any reference would be made to the other's abrupt return from the hotel: he had not seen him since and was puzzled by his cheerfulness. He was inwardly relieved when no mention was made of the matter, and proceeded to lapse into his wonted gloomy silence.

"When's the funeral?" grinned the Cripple. "Don't look like that; you'll spoil the landscape. How does that view strike you? Expand on it; don't keep it all to yourself."

"I've no small talk," said the Pessimist discouragingly.

"Well, unburden your soul. Give us your depressions of life."

"Don't take any notice of him," interposed Brother Anselm. "He's light-headed. He's in love. I'll get a muzzle for him."

The monk was wondering how best to draw out this gloomy being. He knew something already of the man's 'depressions' of life. He determined to discover more of them if he could. He ventured:

"'The Optimist' gave us his views on life the other day. I would very much like to know yours. I should be genuinely interested to hear them. Tell me what you think of the view; and then tell me what you think of life."

"Yes," said the Cripple, "let's be miserable."

"If you wish," replied the Pessimist to Brother Anselm's request. "I never waste words on inane insincerities, and I shall not do so now. I look upon that view as I look upon all that is beautiful; I look upon it as a mockery—a mockery of the hideousness of life."

Even Brother Anselm was startled at the abrupt declaration.

"If life *is* hideous then beauty is mere mockery, I agree. But why hideous?"

"Because it is one long torture of unfulfilled hopes. At its best the world is a fool's paradise; at its worst a slough of despond. You ask me what I think of life. I think life is one huge failure. I am frankly a pessimist. The end of all our efforts is to find happiness. Do we ever find it? We strive and strive, and are baffled at every turn. The conditions of human existence are such that I can see no possibility of life being other than it ever has been—a veritable martyrdom of man."

"You refer," said the monk, "to what are commonly called physical and moral evils? You mean these evils are so overwhelming as to render man's lot more or less unbearable?"

"Just so. I would go even further. I would say that the dominant quality in life *is* evil. I would say that existence itself is evil; that existence is a thing to be abolished."

"Why don't you take poison?" asked the Cripple.

"Because," proceeded the Pessimist, without a vestige of humour, "there is an even worse evil than existence, and that is the will-to-live. My existence affords me the opportunity of inducing my fellow-beings *not* to will to live."

"And supposing the whole human race wills not to live?" Brother Anselm pressed him.

"When it does, then the day will have come to which we pessimists look forward, the day when the human race will cease to propagate itself, and die out."

"To the Day!" The Cripple raised his coffee-cup.

Brother Anselm studied the gloomy being before him. He understood that he was expected to take all this seriously. He asked:

"How many people are there who think as you do? I know Schopenhauer and Hartmann proclaimed pessimism as a philosophical theory, but it was not a very successful venture, was it? You could scarcely say it caught on."

"I admit that there are, alas, very few genuine pessimists."

"Have you ever thought why?"

"I imagine because most people prefer their fool's paradise."

"Hardly," said the monk. "The human race could not everlastingly fool itself. If happiness *were* unattainable men would cease to seek it. Why should they so persistently pursue happiness? Don't you think the very search points to its existence somewhere, to its attainment somehow?"

"I don't see that it points to more than the fact that most men are fools."

"It points to very much more, if your theory is true. If this perpetual quest for happiness is the fool's errand you make of it, then men are worse than fools. They are mad. For it means that human beings have acted irrationally throughout their whole history in a matter vitally concerning their well-being. No, you must reduce your scheme of thinking to its logical conclusion—the perpetual insanity of the human race."

"Call it that, if you like," said the Pessimist. His theories were being pressed further than he cared.

"Right! Then the essential sanity of the human race, which is an axiom of philosophy, is to go; the only sane people are pessimists; and the world is a lunatic asylum—with pessimists for the keepers. Would you subscribe to that?"

The other saw the quandary. . . .

"Hang on, Gloomy, hang on!" goaded the Cripple.

Brother Anselm spared an answer. "May I make one or two remarks about your ideas themselves?"

"Certainly." There was a suggestion of relief.

"Well then, may I suggest that you pessimists are suffering from an obsession—the obsession that evil is the all-pervading thing in this world. It is not. There is just as much, if not more, good than evil. You are so obsessed by your exaggerated notion of evil that you cannot see the good. All the pain and suffering and disease, all the physical evils in the world cannot obliterate the natural happiness inherent in life. Life spells happiness as well as pain. There is health and vigour as well as disease and corruption. There is joy as well as suffering—the mother's joy, the lover's joy, the joys of married love. The very senses of the human body convey innumerable delights—the scent of flowers, the melodies of music, the loveliness of nature, the feel of wind and sunshine. The very intellect of man is a reservoir of gladness. The artist delights to create, the scholar to learn, the scientist to discover. Turn where you will you cannot fail to find happiness of life, as well as pain."

"I cannot deny that," said the Pessimist. "I admit that there is a transitory happiness which men squeeze out of life. But how long does it last? The joys you mention are but coloured bubbles. When grasped they burst—and life once more is emptiness."

"True—of worldly happiness," the monk replied. "The things of earth perish: they cannot permanently satisfy. But why should that make men despair? Why shouldn't it be a stern reminder that permanent happiness lies elsewhere? You pessimists demand of this world what it can never give; what it was never meant to give. When your demand is refused you find refuge in despair, and turn upon life. In other words you—sulk."

The other retorted hotly: "If there were a guarantee of permanent happiness somewhere, then there would be no cause for complaint!"

"*If* there were a guarantee!" exclaimed Brother Anselm. "Look here, you and your co-pessimists are not so blind as all that. You know well enough that there is such a thing in this world as the Catholic Church. You can't overlook her; she's too big, too unique. You *must* know that she guarantees the very thing you ask of life, the very thing you blame the world for refusing. But have you so much as glanced at her guarantee? Have you even examined her claims? She comes open-handed; she shows her credentials. For two thousand years her millions have satisfied themselves that she can do what she promises—lead them to full unending happiness. Until you take the trouble to inquire of her, your complaint is a sheer pretence. I'm sorry, but you brought this on yourself. I simply couldn't let your remark pass."

"Pretence?" The Pessimist looked hurt.

"Yes, *pretence.* I use the word deliberately. I want you to see the insincerity, conscious or unconscious, of the pessimistic attitude. It is insincere to ignore the Catholic Church when she offers the very thing you ask for. It suggests that pessimism is a mere posture. When you can come to me and say: 'There is no guarantee of any final happiness. The Catholic Church lies. I have proved her claims false, her promises a hoax'—if ever you come and look me in the face and say that, then I will say to you: 'You may go now in all sincerity—and wallow in your slough of despond.'"

§ 2

In so far as the Pessimist enjoyed anything at all, he en-joyed a discussion—provided it was confined to vague gener-alities. But Brother Anselm would not allow any vagueness. His direct method of driving home concrete facts and realities was decidedly disconcerting. Brother Anselm had a way, too, of looking *into* you while he did it. You found yourself penetrated by a pair of deep-set grey eyes—compelling you to be perfectly honest with him, and with yourself. He had flung a challenge; and the Pessimist knew it for a fair challenge. The Catholic Church gave the lie to pessimism. Her assertions could not be swept aside as beneath consideration. She was too potent a factor in the lives of men for that. He knew enough of her to know that she did make life worth living for her millions. She not merely said a thing: she did it. She sent her thousands daily into eternity radiant with hope. "Existence is a thing to be abolished!" His declamation suddenly sounded hollow and melodramatic. He was glad the monk had ignored it. . . .

"Your Despondency ruminates." The Cripple broke in upon these considerations.

"I am unwillingly admitting to myself that Brother Anselm's challenge is a fair one," replied the Pessimist. "I am going to put an equally fair one to him—a sort of counter-challenge."

He turned to the monk.

"You admit there is a vast amount of pain and suffering and evil in the world; physical and moral evils you called them. And, according to you, God is the cause of all things. He is therefore the cause of these evils. Would you then tell me why you call Him a *good* God?"

Brother Anselm picked up the glove without hesitation.

"There is no question, in any case, of God not being good. If God were not good there would be no such thing as goodness in the world—goodness can only come from God: there's nothing else for it to come from. Also, if God were not good, He wouldn't *be* God. God is Infinite Being, and must therefore contain within Himself all the perfections of being in an infinite degree. If there is goodness in creatures, as I imagine even you would admit, then there must be infinite goodness in God. He must be infinitely good."

"But that's metaphysics!" exclaimed the Pessimist, alarmed.

"Of course it's metaphysics. Why not? Metaphysics is the science for putting your mind right on these matters, just as physics are the right thing for putting your liver right. Most of the wrong thinking of today is due to neglect of metaphysics. However, that's by the way——"

"And it doesn't answer my challenge."

"Give me a chance," smiled the monk. "I want to answer your points in the right order. Now comes your question of God being the cause of all things, including evil. My answer is—evil is not a thing."

"Not a thing! What do you mean?"

"It is not a thing in itself."

Brother Anselm suddenly stood up. He proceeded to place his big figure between the line of the sun and the Pessimist, so that his shadow fell on him.

"Now, look. Is my shadow——"

"Watch him, Gloomy. It's all done by kindness"—from the ambulance.

"——Is my shadow, in which you are sitting, a thing in itself?"

The Pessimist looked perplexed.

"I must confess I'm in the dark."

"Because I'm in the light," said Brother Anselm. "I am an obstacle in the way of the sun. You are sitting in an absence of sunlight, called a shadow. The shadow is not a thing in itself. It is an absence of light."

The monk sat down. Applause from the Cripple.

"Got it, Gloomy? See if you can do it!"

"*You'll* be smacked and taken home in the pram," said Brother Anselm. "Now. . . . Evil is like that shadow. God does not cause evil any more than the sun caused that shadow. Neither is evil a thing in itself any more than the shadow is. God radiates nothing but goodness, just as the sun radiates nothing but light. But He allows obstacles to get in the way of His goodness. And then, what happens? You get an absence of goodness—called evil."

"Then God allows evil?" The Pessimist sounded more hopeful.

"Certainly. But, mind you, in the physical realm this absence of goodness is not strictly an evil at all. It is merely a failure to attain perfection—disease is a failure to attain perfect health. Why shouldn't there be failures in Nature? This universe is finite and therefore limited in perfection. I would go even further—why shouldn't this world be all the better for some things failing? Why shouldn't it be all the better for pain and suffering? Don't you think the Christian revelation gives us a glimpse of the immense value of suffering?"

"If it is true—of human suffering, yes; but not of animal suffering."

"How do you know animals *do* suffer?" said Brother Anselm. "Certainly they do not know pain as we do. Their bodily organization is far simpler than ours. Neither have they rational minds like ours to intensify pain. They are not self-conscious like us. The yelping of a dog being whipped does not necessarily mean pain; it may merely mean a reaction to what is bad for its body. Animal suffering is enormously exaggerated. Judged by the sentiments of some people animal life might almost be a cruel joke. Normally it is anything but painful; it is rapturously happy. However, when it comes to the question of why animals should suffer at all, if they do, then I admit that, beyond teaching self-preservation, the place of animal suffering cannot be seen clearly. Suffering, all suffering is a mystery; I don't deny it. That, of course, is merely because we don't know God's eternal plan. Our understanding is very limited. All the more reason for trusting the Almighty."

"Um!" said the Pessimist. "That seems to me like asking people to shut their eyes to what is evil in the plan, and go on trusting blindly."

"No, no—the reverse. I am trying to open your eyes to what is *not* evil in the plan—pain and suffering. At the same time I am certainly asking you to accept the limitations of your finite mind, if you call that 'trusting blindly.' It is the world that shuts its eyes to *evil*—moral evil, sin." Brother Anselm paused. "Now this is what I want to say.—Sin is the only real evil. *That* is not in the plan, but in man. God could not plan sin. If He could, He would be the cause of it, as your challenge implied. Sin is man's rejection of God. God could not will the rejection of Himself: He cannot be the cause of sin."

The Pessimist stuck to his guns: "But if He is the cause of man He is the cause of what a man does."

"That depends," said the monk. "God is the cause of man, yes. He is the cause, too, of man's free-will; also of what a man is intended to produce—goodness. But He is not the cause of man's failure to produce goodness—called sin. Sin is man's failure, not God's. It is due to the misuse of man's free-will."

The Pessimist considered.

"No," he said, "perhaps I was wrong. You don't ask people to shut their eyes; you ask them to shut their mouths."

It was his first attempt at humour. Brother Anselm laughed. "In the sense of not opening them to criticize the Almighty, yes."

The Pessimist considered again.

"You people have no occasion to criticize: you have faith."

"Faith, of course, is everything," replied the monk. "And it is given to all who ask. But even faith does not solve every problem. It enables us to assent to what God has revealed. It is not an *open sesame* to all the problems of life. We Catholics *might* start criticizing the Deity for not revealing more. . . . What happens to unbaptized infants? God has chosen to leave their lot veiled in mystery. Are we then to become suspicious? Are we to shake our fists at heaven? Such an attitude would be not merely blasphemous, it would be stupid and irrational. God created those babes solely out of love. He created them to be immortal. Cannot we trust their immortal state to the Love that gave them being? . . . That is only one example. You see what I mean? We simply *must* trust. Any other attitude would be folly."

"There are problems then for all?" The Pessimist's attitude was softening.

"No," answered Brother Anselm. "There are no problems for anybody really."

"How do you mean?"

"There are no problems for God, because He understands. There are no problems for us, because we are not meant to understand—at present. The only problems are those men make for themselves."

Brother Anselm put his hand on the other's shoulder.

"There are mysteries though. And one of them is a shadow that falls upon the earth. It was that shadow, at its darkest, that fell upon Him Who *made* the earth. He has never allowed that shadow to fall upon His children as it fell upon Himself. He has never asked them to suffer what He suffered Himself as Man. . . . Don't you think He understands? Don't you think we may leave His creation to Him?"

The Pessimist walked across to the parapet and stood there with his arms folded. He remained wrapped in thought. Suddenly he turned round and faced the Cripple.

"I want to ask you something extremely personal. I am slow to change my opinions. A comparatively brief discussion is not sufficient justification for doing so. Whether I change them eventually may depend a good deal on you—on what you say now. Of course you may not care to answer me——"

"I'll answer you on one condition," the Cripple replied.

"Yes?"

"That you will free yourself from the influence of—of a certain person. I have decided to do so myself. You know whom I mean."

The Pessimist thought for a moment. He had seen that malicious influence at work, and its effects....

"Yes, I can promise that."

"Fire away, then."

He took stock of the Cripple, and then said: "My question may be embarrassing to you, but your answer may be enlightening to me. It is this. You are a test-case for my theory of life, if I may put it like that. You are one of life's victims. You, if any, I should say have cause to despair. Does my idea of life ring true to you?... Now, does it?"

The Cripple replied without hesitation: "No, it does not. It rings false—utterly false. I must admit—I'm ashamed of it—that I did adopt the policy of despair at first; partly under influence. But somebody worked day and night to save me from myself— and he's done it. Despair is the refuge of cowards and shirkers; I'm certain of it. It demoralizes. It unmans, paralyses; it draws out all that is worst in a man. It made me behave like a low-down cad. The slough of despond has become loathsome to me."

"Brother Anselm's—er—strong personality has undoubtedly influenced you; I can certainly see that."

"It isn't only that," said the Cripple. "It's what he says. It appeals to me—to my reason. It rings true. You wonder if it *is* true. I believe it is. I only know that it has made life worth living again. I've—I've sort of put my hand in God's; and I'm happy."

The Pessimist's reply was checked by Brother Anselm. "Don't say now whether you believe me or not; my—er—strong personality might influence your decision. Instead, tell me what made you a pessimist."

"The War," replied the other.

"Funny!" said Brother Anselm. "It made me a monk."

The Cripple pricked up his ears.

"Were *you* in the War?"

"I was. Battery doctor—Gunners," replied Brother Anselm.

"Good gracious! . . . You never told me. I say, we must have a pow-wow about all this. . . . Did you get through all right?"

"Looks like it."

"Did you get knocked out?"

"Rather!—inside out; all to bits. Brought back in a jug."

"No, but seriously?"

"Well, hardly knocked out. I was wounded, though."

"How——"

The Cripple stopped short. There was a look about Brother Anselm which told him not to ask more. . . . He felt mystified. It was the second time the monk had pulled him up like this.

They drove back in the twilight down the long winding road. Nearing the monastery gates another car overtook and passed them in a whirl of dust, but not before Brother Anselm had caught a glimpse of its occupant—leaning forward to observe the Cripple on his stretcher. It was the Atheist! . . . There was an unpleasant smile on his face. The monk did not like that smile.

He did not tell the Cripple whom he had seen.

Chapter VIII

The Major at the Monastery

"I REMEMBER him well," said the Major. "Good-looking boy—fair hair. He wasn't in my battery; but I used to run into him pretty often. Poor devil! Poor devil! . . . Up at some monastery place? I'll go and see him."

"I'll take you there myself," said the Atheist.

An unexpected opportunity of getting in touch with the Cripple had presented itself. Except for that fleeting glimpse from his car the Atheist had not seen him since his return to the monastery a week ago. His instinct had told him he would not be welcome there. However, common courtesy would prevent any unpleasantness on the monk's part if he appeared in the rôle of the Major's friend. Good manners obviously demanded that he should conduct him there on his visit of sympathy, and present him to the Cripple.

Most timely! The Major and he had met and recognized each other in the hotel lounge, half an hour before. Their last meeting had been at the front during the War. As Gunners' officers they had served in the same battery.

"Are you all right again yourself?" asked the Major, interrupting his thoughts. "You were nearly done in, weren't you—that night on the ridge? I never saw you again after that wipe-out. Er—did you ever find out who it was—the man who got you back?"

"No," said the Atheist. "I never saw him. I was unconscious.

He seems to have got me down to the dressing-station before I came round. That was all I could discover."

"I found out later who it was," said the Major in a guarded tone.

"Did you?. . . Who was it? Why didn't you let me know?"

"I was not allowed to," the Major replied. "He asked me *not* to let you know."

"Oh!. . . But surely you can tell me now."

"No, I don't think I can. He made me promise. As far as I can see I am still bound by that promise. I haven't seen him since the War. I only asked whether you knew because I thought you might have found out yourself."

"Oh well," said the Atheist, "if you can't, I won't press you further. But I wonder why he didn't want me to know."

"Yes," meditated the Major. "I wonder why."

The following afternoon they started off for the monastery. They left the road half-way up for the path across the fields. The Atheist thought that by entering the grounds at the side of the monastery they could reach the garden, where the Cripple would probably be, leaving Brother Anselm unaware of their arrival. In that case he might get a few minutes alone with the Cripple: it could be suggested to the Major that he should look over the monastery and the church, famous for their architectural beauty.

His surmise was correct. As they entered the garden the Cripple could be seen in his ambulance under the trees—and alone. He was reading a book. It seemed to absorb his attention; for the two had almost reached him, before he looked up. He regarded them for a moment with surprise—a perceptible annoyance clouding his face as he saw the Atheist.

"Well, do you remember me?" said the Major.

The Cripple looked hard at him. The annoyance changed to a smile of recognition.

"My dear Major! . . . Yes, it's you! Where on earth have you blown from?"

The Major proceeded to account for his sudden appearance. The Atheist fetched a chair from the arbour, and the other sat down at the Cripple's side. There would be no chance yet, he thought; these two must have their talk first. He strolled about examining the flowers. There was an unpleasant look on his face. He had noticed the Cripple's annoyance at seeing him. He had also noticed the book he was reading. It was a religious one.

The Major and the Cripple were soon engaged in animated conversation, recalling old times—the days with the Gunners at the front. Twenty minutes passed. The Atheist began to get impatient. The monk might turn up at any moment. . . .

"I'm anxious that you should look round the monastery and church. They're very fine specimens—fifteenth century."

"Eh, what?" said the Major. "Oh, I don't know. I'm not much of a hand at architecture. I'd sooner have a pow-wow here, I think."

The Atheist tried again:

"Come for a moment, then, and get a view from over there."

"Excuse me," said the Major to the Cripple.

When they were out of earshot the Atheist put his hand on the Major's shoulder: "Would you let me have a few minutes alone with him? Something confidential, you know."

"Certainly, certainly," agreed the Major. "I'll look round for a bit at the monkery. Fifth century, you said?"

"Fifteenth," replied the Atheist. He walked back towards the Cripple.

"Make a fine barracks that!" said the Major to himself, surveying the great front of the monastery. As he stood there a side door opened. A monk came out and walked in his direction. The Major raised his hat as he approached—and then stared. Brother Anselm (for it was he) bowed—and stared too. Then simultaneously they stretched out hands. . . .

"Well, I'm damned!" exclaimed the Major. "It's the Doc! . . ."

He gripped again.

"Heavens alive, man! After all these ages! . . . Yes, it's the Doc! . . . But what—what *are* you doing here? What's this get-up?"

"I'm a monk now."

"Hold me up!" said the Major. "It'll take a couple of stiffs to bring me round."

Brother Anselm laughed and put his arm through the other's.

"Dear old Major! It's awfully good to see you again. But what are *you* doing here? Going to join the Order?"

They sat down on a bench near by and began questioning each other. The Major related his meeting with the Atheist at the hotel and his discovery of the Cripple. Brother Anselm had never come across the Cripple at the front? No. He would like to know more about the accident. He couldn't quite make out the Atheist——

"He never told me you were here."

"He doesn't remember me," said Brother Anselm. "He has never recognized me; though I knew him at once—the night of the accident. He knew me very little out there. But I knew *him* rather well, you see."

"And didn't much care for him, if I remember right. I could never quite make him out myself; though he was pleasant enough in the mess."

"Oh yes, he was pleasant enough."

"I wonder why you—why you—well, you know. . . ."

"Never mind that!" said Brother Anselm. His grey eyes searched the Major. "Remember your promise still binds. You remember it, don't you?"

"I do. I had to remember it yesterday. We were talking about that night. He has never found out——"

"Don't let him know you knew me out there." Brother Anselm sounded peremptory.

"Doc, you're the——"

"Cut it, man, cut it! Er—I might as well mention that he and I are not on the best of terms."

"That so?" replied the Major. "He didn't seem to mind coming up here—insisted on bringing me himself."

"Bringing you? Is he here now?"

"In that garden part, yes. He wanted a few minutes with—— What's the matter?"

Brother Anselm had suddenly risen and was looking in the direction of the garden. His face had become grave. . . .

"If you don't mind," he said, "I think we'll join them."

"The devil!" muttered the Major. "There's going to be trouble."

Chapter IX

Brother Anselm and the Atheist

THE MAJOR followed Brother Anselm through the grounds. The monk walked quickly and seemed almost to have forgotten his presence. As they entered the garden it became apparent that trouble of some kind had already begun. A high-pitched voice was audible. They came into the open of the lawn. Under the trees at the other end the Atheist was standing, back to them, in a nonchalant attitude, surveying the Cripple who was flushed with anger. He was plainly resenting something the Atheist had said.

"You can go and take your lies with you! They're not wanted here. He knows a darned sight more about religion than you do. You——"

"Good afternoon," said Brother Anselm. The Atheist wheeled round. For a fraction of a second he was nonplussed— but no more.

"Good afternoon." And he held out his hand.

Brother Anselm did not notice it; his look was on the Cripple. There was a strained silence. The Major blew his nose. . . .

"Perhaps"—Brother Anselm turned to the Atheist—"perhaps you would be wiser to go."

An unpleasant glint appeared in the other's eyes.

"Thank you for your courteous suggestion."

"And you for your courteous intrusion," replied the monk.

The Atheist hesitated. . . . His departure would be an acknowledgment of defeat. It would make him look an utter fool in the Major's eyes. . . . He assumed indifference.

"Oh well, I have no desire to trespass on anybody's preserves. And, of course, your neophyte in religion requires careful protection. I always understood hot-house treatment was the best. I suppose religion is too fragile to be exposed to the breath of criticism."

"Don't imagine," said Brother Anselm unruffled, "that my suggestion indicated any fear for my 'neophyte's' religion. I should say from what I heard that he is quite capable of looking after it himself. If by 'criticism' you mean your own lying arguments, may I remind you that you train yourself to the finger-tips in those arguments and then take a mean advantage of those who have not even studied them. You deliberately schemed to work off your stuff on him in my absence. However, I am here now—if you wish me to deal with you."

The Atheist just managed to check his anger.

"Am I to understand that you withdraw your suggestion that I should go? You would like to——"

"I never suggested you *should* go: I said you would be *wiser* to go."

The other failed to appreciate the significance of the remark; but instead saw a chance of saving his pride—also of humiliating the monk. He would stop and—yes, a monk would be easy. . . . He would be gracious.

"I must ask your pardon for misunderstanding you. I don't wish for any unpleasantness myself. May I remark that you misjudged me in supposing that I reserved myself for neophytes. Let me put to *you* what I was saying to our friend——"

Brother Anselm turned to the Major. "I must apologise for inflicting this on you. I have given this—gentleman a chance to leave; since he refuses his chance I shall take mine of letting him know exactly what I think of him."

He turned back to the Atheist—

"Please don't think that I am going to enter into an argument with you, at any rate of the kind you are hoping for. It would be a waste of breath. You hate religion and you hate God. I doubt if you even believe your own lies against His existence; you pay too much attention to Him to disbelieve in Him. You hate Him too much. Men don't hate what doesn't exist."

This was the reverse of what the Atheist wanted. He had hoped to draw the monk and then make him look foolish by ridiculing his arguments. Instead he was being lashed with scorn. He flared out:

"You're infernally rude, sir. I didn't stay here to be insulted."

"You are at liberty to go whenever you like. That's the way—across the fields."

The Atheist looked at the others. The Major was lighting a cigarette uncomfortably; the Cripple watching Brother Anselm. He felt maddened at being humiliated before them; exasperated by his inability to get to grips with the monk. If he went now, it would be like a whipped cur slinking off. No, he couldn't. . . .

"Very well," said Brother Anselm. "You choose to stay. So you pretend that I am insulting you. I wish I were. Unfortunately I know you better than you are aware of. You deserve far more than you are getting: you deserve no mercy. I have in my mind at this moment the havoc you have worked with your glib tongue. The crime of murder is light compared with the perpetual crime in which you are engaged. A murderer of bodies is harmless compared with a murderer of souls. Your life is one long endeavour to strangle religion in every soul that you can. That is how you work off your venom against the God Who made you."

"You——" Fury had mastered the Atheist now. He forgot a momentary bewilderment at the monk's knowledge of him.

"You—and your God! Show me your God, and don't fling Him at me until you can. Fetch Him from His heaven! You priests find it convenient to keep Him up there, out of sight. You're wise. He's safer there. You can excuse His silence when He's far away—conceal His absence, can't you?"

The sneer failed to affect Brother Anselm. He had himself well in hand. He continued in the same deliberate way:

"Yes, my friend, God *is* silent to you, and such as you. He *is* absent from you. You don't want Him. You would hardly expect Him to force Himself upon you as you force your hatred of Him upon others. He treats even His enemies with courtesy."

"Words! Mere words!—'You and such as you!' Really! And what about the world? Does He condescend to give it a sign of His presence?"

"Would you condescend to notice if He did?" said the monk. "So He keeps in His heaven? He never gives a sign? We never show you God? Indeed! Have you ever heard of the Incarnation?... When He does the very thing you defy Him to do you refuse to believe it. You ask for a sign of His presence: when He gives one you call it a fable. You challenge us to show Him: the Catholic Church has been doing so for two thousand years. You scoff at His silence: when He speaks you deride His revelation. You won't have His Incarnation. Very well.... If you can conceive of any better way in which God could show Himself than by becoming Man, any better way of speaking than through human lips, any better way of being present to the world than in human form—if you can, would you suggest it?..."

Brother Anselm waited. No answer came. The Atheist looked about irresolutely....

"You have no suggestion to offer?... You still choose to stay?"

The monk resumed in the same level tone:

"Very well. I've more for you. You said something about us excusing God's silence. Do you think we need to? Do you think God *is* silent—to us Catholics? Do you think all our millions have no experience of God? Do you suppose that all the scientists and philosophers, the great thinkers of the world, who have been and are Catholics today—do you suppose they are all so many victims of priestcraft, terrified by mediæval moonshine, blindly believing in a God they never know? Do you think that we could assent to the mysteries of our faith if God were silent to our souls? Do you know that God is Personally present to each one of us—as a Personal God of love?... If I could summon all our legions from the ages of the past, they would thunder back in unison the truth of what I say."

The Atheist found his tongue again.

"Delightful credulity! Do you expect me to believe this childish nonsense?"

"Scarcely. You are not fit to believe it. I am telling you what *we* believe."

"You may believe what you like; your 'Personal God of love' won't stir a finger when it comes to the test—when you suffer, when disease and pain get hold of you. You may pray at Him then until you are black in the face. Your God has a wonderful way of showing His love!"

The Cripple suddenly fired out: "You leave God's love alone! He can love a rotter like me; I know that much, or I couldn't carry on. . . . Yes, I'm carrying on in spite of you."

So that was why he had lost his hold on the Cripple, thought the Atheist. It was not merely the monk who had done it. The Cripple himself had decided against him. It roused his malice even further. He hated failing.

"Your susceptibility to superstition is contemptible."

"Also your spite," said Brother Anselm. "So you imagine us whining and squirming before God to be released from pain and suffering—and God taking no notice. You fling that at us for the folly of trusting His love? Would you believe me if I said that we don't expect Him to make things easy for us? We don't. We expect pain and suffering——"

"I always thought Christians were fools."

"——And you implied that God does not evidence His love for us. Are you or we the ones to judge of that? Do you think we could serve others for the love of God, as we do, if God did not first love us—if we didn't know it?. . . . Have you ever heard of the Crucifixion?"

"You may keep your religion to yourself!—to yourself! Do you hear?"

"You needn't shout at me. I am not deaf," replied Brother Anselm. "I shall not keep my religion to myself. My religion is my answer to you. You shall know why we love God; and you shall know God's love for us. . . . Do you see this Crucifix I wear? Do you know what that means? Yes, look at it! . . . That is why we love God. And that is God's love for us. That is why we expect pain and suffering——"

"I said you could keep your religion to yourself!"

"I know; I heard you. I am not surprised. The very naming of the Cross is repugnant to you. You are afraid of it. It proclaims you and your kind for what you are—liars. You profess to ask for a sign of a God of love. When God reveals on the Cross His infinite love for you, you deny it. You fling it back in His face, and spit on your crucified Saviour."

Brother Anselm paused.

He then went up close to the Atheist and looked him square in the eyes. It was open war now between two powerful personalities. The monk was the calmer. The Atheist was breathing hard, clenching and unclenching his fingers in a state of nervous hesitancy. . . .

"That is all I am going to say to you now. I have said it that you may know Whom you libel. I have also said it that you may know yourself and what you are, and your own vileness, and your dirty work——"

"Damn you! you bloody monk! . . ."

"No, you don't," said Brother Anselm, catching him by the wrist. The Atheist had tried to strike him.

The Major sprang up to interfere. Brother Anselm, however, seemed capable of looking after himself. He loosed his grip and the other's arm dropped. . . .

The Major felt something must be done. He went up to the Atheist and led him a few yards away. "Take my advice and go. It's no good. You're making a fool of yourself."

For a moment the Atheist stood there angrily conscious that he had lost all semblance of dignity. Then suddenly he whipped round—and walked off.

The abrupt climax left the others speechless, staring after the retreating figure. The Major, after a while, lit a cigarette. His hands were trembling.

"It's not my business, but why did you go at him like that?"

"I'm sorry, you two," Brother Anselm replied. "There was nothing else for it. Nothing else could have any effect on him, but a moral horse-whipping. I hated doing it; but his only chance is to realize what he is." There was no suggestion of triumph; more of sadness.

"Queer thing religion," said the Major. "Devilish queer! So that's why you weren't fond of him in the War—over religion."

The Cripple roused himself.

"Was it in the War you knew him?"

"It was," replied Brother Anselm. "He was in the same battery as myself. He's forgotten me, though."

"Good gracious! That was it?" The Cripple thought for a moment. "I see now. . . ."

"There's something else you don't know yet," said the Major.

"What's that?" asked the Cripple.

"Brother Anselm was my battery Doc."

The Cripple slowly took it in. "Well, I'm hanged! . . ."

"And I'd very much like to tell you something more about him——"

"There'll be trouble if you do." The monk stopped him just in time.

The Cripple looked curious; but refrained from asking questions. "So you were all three in the same battery. What a rum world!"

"Mighty rum!" said the Major. "And you'd think it rummier still, if this villain of a monk would let me speak."

He laid his hand affectionately on Brother Anselm's shoulder.

Chapter X

A Thing That Had to be Done

BROTHER ANSELM closed his breviary. He had finished the Office for the day in his cell, an unforeseen occurrence having prevented him attending Choir with the other monks.

After the Major's departure the Cripple had said something about not feeling well. Brother Anselm had taken him back to bed, and then for an hour or more he had watched him through an agony of stabbing, torturing pain. Throughout no word of complaint had escaped his lips. Brother Anselm had noticed his eyes resting at times on the Crucifix hanging on the wall. When the attack had passed the Cripple had lain quiet for a little, and then asked him a curiously direct question: "Supposing you were in my position; supposing you knew that you had to lie on your back for the rest of your days, cut off from the pleasures of life, and having at times to suffer pain like this—how exactly would you take it?" Brother Anselm had looked at the youthful face all drawn and white, and then through the window into the distance where the sun was sinking into long lines of purple, before he answered. "How would I take it? I would take it as an honour—an honour to be chosen for the royal road of pain; and I would take it as a privilege, to be asked to share so fully the Cross with Christ." And the Cripple had just said—" Thank you."

He was now in a sleep of sheer exhaustion.

A Thing That Had to be Done

Brother Anselm laid his breviary on the table.

He rested his chin on his hand and looked out into the night. The evening star had not yet set. It hung there twinkling, crystalled in the deepening blue. His mind turned to the events of the afternoon. He could feel no regret for what he had said to the Atheist. It might have some effect. It might have none. In the latter case, and if he gave further trouble, there was only one way left of bringing him to shame—to that shame of himself without which he would never change. Yes, one way was left.

He was thankful now that the other had not remembered him as doctor of the battery, thankful too that he had never found out who had saved his life. For the other's ignorance left him in possession of a powerful moral weapon to use, if necessary; much though he disliked the idea of using it at all.

As he looked out into the peace of the night, another night recalled itself. A night at the front; a night of horrors—the night on which he had saved the Atheist's life.

The vivid memory of it all came back:

. . . They were retreating; had been retreating for two days. An order had come through on the second afternoon. Their guns were to hold a section of the line, unless compelled to retire. The enemy had broken through two miles ahead. He could see the Major now, standing there with the G.H.Q. chit in his hands, looking grave as he folded it and remarking: "That means hell. Get to work, Captain!"—and to himself: "Doc, you'd better stay here; you'll be wanted soon." For an hour or so their guns were letting loose, until he was nearly deaf from the incessant roaring bark. Once the Major had come back to the dug-out: "Won't be long now, Doc. They'll pay this back double." It was his signal.

As he climbed up into the open there came the slow, steady whistle of a delay-fuse. . . . Crump! Dead on their line. Then those guns six miles away got to work. The Major was right; it was going to be hell. The relentless shells crashed unceasingly, mercilessly, shaking the ground under his feet with their cavernous thunder, flinging up sods by the ton.

Two direct gun-hits; and his own work began. Those mangled heaps that had been men did not need attention: they were silenced like their guns. He told the dead at a glance. The wounded took all his time. Once something red-hot seemed to be drawn across his forehead. A bit of shell had grazed him. He ignored it until the blood ran down into his eyes; then told the man whose leg he was bandaging to do the same for his own head. He went on in a sort of mechanical way patching them up one by one, vaguely aware that his work was more or less futile; for the wounded themselves were being killed off now. The stretcher-bearers were doing their utmost, but it was impossible to cope with the havoc of this cruel barrage. The air was thick with the smell of smoke and blood. He wondered when the Major would give the order to retire. They would be wiped out before long. It was getting dark, too. The flaming explosions were now lighting up the white, staring faces of the gunners. They were working the guns still in action in a sort of mad, hopeless way; listening amidst the din, like himself, for the word that meant release.

It came at last—that order. Then the clanking of harness and the drivers cursing their horses up the hill, guns being hitched and pulled off at a gallop, the tattered remnant of gunners hurriedly following—nervous to leave the hell-spot.

The Major remained there peering about him. "Seen the Captain, Doc?" No, he had not; but supposed he was with the gunners. The other seemed satisfied. He saw the rest of the wounded taken away, then joined the Major. They lit a cigarette each, took a last look at that scene of devastation, and made their way down to the waggon-lines. There the Major received another order from G.H.Q. They were to retire to a position four miles back. Their infantry-lines had been broken through again. The enemy was only a mile away.

The Major was asking for the Captain: he could not be found. "Seen him yet, Doc?" No, not a sign, he had replied. They must clear off anyway, said the Major; and he went to attend to the guns and waggons. A gunner came up—could he speak to the Doctor? He had seen the Captain knocked out close to his own gun; his leg was broken, he believed—thought he had been taken to the dressing-station. . . .

(Brother Anselm remembered those next few minutes very clearly.)

. . . He suddenly understood. He knew quite well that the Captain had *not* been taken to the dressing-station; that he must have been overlooked, and left up there amongst the horrors of that death-trap. He walked away from the shouting and noise of the battery preparing to start, and in the darkness strained his eyes to make out their recent position. Yes, he could see the rise of the hill, the lurid glare of shell-bursts revealing it in black outline. The Captain was there—somewhere. . . .

He paced about in an agony of indecision.

There was no obligation upon him to do it. Why should he? Why should he try to save a man against whose vile, lying ways his whole being revolted—merely to give him further opportunities? He had discovered his evil influence in the battery already, and the Captain had only been a few weeks with them. They had scarcely crossed each other's paths; for his work as medical officer took him away from the mess for most of the day. But he had heard sufficient to know that all the Captain's spare time was spent in trying to instil unbelief and even malice against God into others—he had a way with him, it seemed, that made them listen. . . . No, he couldn't. . . . Oh, why that man of all men?. . . But left there to die like a dog with all that infamy upon him? Could he?. . . He couldn't leave him like that. Suddenly he knew he would do it.

He found his batmen holding his horse ready; the battery was on the point of starting. He ascertained from another officer their next position; then, after swinging himself into the saddle, he leant down to his batman: "Tell the Major I'll get there on my own, see?" The batman saluted and disappeared.

He dug with his heels and rode out of the turmoil round to the right, as if going on in advance. As soon as the darkness hid him from sight, he wheeled his horse round. "No, you don't!"— and he dug at its sides until the unwilling beast plunged forward, and then sidled along the road whinnying to its companions in the dark. "Shut up! . . . Sorry, my beauty, but it's got to be done. Come on!" He patted the horse's neck and urged it into a canter. His eyes were growing used to the dark, and the white of the road made going fairly easy. After half a mile he pulled up, searching for the track up the hill to the left. He found it. The hard clatter of the road changed to the squelch of mud. "Quietly! don't put us down!" Half-way up he dismounted. Shells were dropping again and there were too many holes. He led his horse carefully until they reached the top. There he halted and took his bearings. On the right a quarter of a mile away he could just see the line of the road running over the hill. There were figures against the horizon hurrying along—their infantry, he guessed. Fritz must be pretty close. Now, which was his way? That was the line of dug-outs. Where had the guns——

This one was coming a bit too—— "Steady now! . . ." A blinding flash! The ground heaved up with a deafening roar. He felt himself almost lifted, and then flung down half-buried in mud and sods—choking to get his breath. . . . He waited; then gradually freed himself and struggled to his feet—dazed and shaking. It was all blinding smoke. . . . His horse?. . . That dark bulk lying there? He slowly perceived what had happened. The horse had taken the shell, blast and all—and saved him. It was dead. He looked at it with a pang. His hand was dripping, running with blood. It was from his arm. He took off his tunic, found some bandages in the pocket, and with teeth and fingers bound up the wound. It was a nasty gash. He succeeded in nearly staying the flow.

"Now, get on with it!" Where had those guns been? Another shell-burst lit up the scene for a second and gave him a glimpse of gun wreckage a hundred yards ahead. He went forward carefully avoiding shell-holes, and reached what had been their gun-line. It would be somewhere along here.

He put his hands to his mouth, shouted the Captain's name, and listened. An eerie silence followed. He tried again. . . . Only the wind answered, sweeping over the ridge to mock his effort. He would have to search then, amongst the dead. Gruesome job; but it had to be done. He began at the far end, picking his way among them—some with faces turned to heaven, some to earth—looking closely for three stars on the shoulder-strap. He came to a group of three lying close to a twisted gun-wheel. As he bent down his doctor's intuition told him that the one in the middle was—not a corpse. There were three stars on the shoulder-strap. He struck a match. A gust of wind blew it out; but not before he had recognized—the Captain!

The cynical twist of the mouth was what he had seen. It was enough. He was alive, but unconscious; evidently from loss of blood. The left leg was broken and the puttee still oozing warmly. That must be stopped. He wound his remaining bandages round tightly above the wet part. The Captain began to mutter unintelligibly and then lapsed again into unconsciousness.

If he had had his horse! He could have managed fairly well then. It would be no easy matter carrying this helpless man over the shell-riddled ground. The strain of the last few hours combined with his recent experience and loss of blood was beginning to tell on him. But it had to be done. About four hundred yards he guessed it would be to the nearest point of the road, keeping along the ridge.

He knelt and hauled the Captain's body on to his back with his arms dangling over his shoulders; then, gripping the wrists, struggled to his feet and started. He got clear of the wreckage and corpses. He wished those shells would stop; they were landing now between him and the road. They didn't matter to himself—he had got to a stage when nothing seemed to matter—but he had to get the Captain back. He staggered on. . . . He must be half-way. They were bursting close now. Clods of earth were hitting him. He set his teeth. His head began to feel funny—silly. Everything seemed to be aiming at him. There were lights dancing. . . . "Don't be a fool! get on with it, man!" It had to be done. With a fierce effort of will he went on. Then he began to lurch about. The Captain was getting heavier. . . . The ground was coming at him. . . .

He regained consciousness to find himself and the Captain lying in a shell-hole. With great difficulty he sat up—dizzy and sick, vaguely realizing that he had collapsed. He was played-out. His forehead and arm were both bleeding again. He tried to stand; but his head whizzed, and he sank back in a stupid, feeble way. The Captain was talking deliriously to himself, roused by the shock of the fall. He pulled him into an easier position, lay still to recover a little, and then, dragging himself up painfully on hands and knees, managed to crawl over the edge of the shell-hole.

The moon was coming up above the line of the ridge, revealing the hideous desolation all round—cavities and tree-stumps standing out blackly against the pale light. There was something white near by. Was it——? Yes, it was the road. He had nearly done it, then! He followed the white track with aching eyes. It was empty now of those hurrying figures. . . . No, it was not. There were some men scurrying along—only a hundred yards away! He shouted. . . .

The sharp whistle of a shell came, and he saw them crouching for the burst. Then two more—and they were running to get out of range. They had not heard him. . . .

He watched their figures recede into the distance and disappear. A sense of helplessness came upon him. He searched the road again. Not a soul in sight; only those ghostly tree-stumps everywhere. He looked down at the Captain lying there. . . . A thought came to him. Without that burden. . . . "You blackguard! you blackguard! No, you don't. You get back with him, or you don't get back at all."

He was too weak now to carry the Captain a yard further. He could only watch the road for any help that might appear. The feeling of isolation increased. Not a living being about. Nothing but death here. Dead stumps, dead bodies, dead—— Something arrested his eyes.

Curious he hadn't seen it before! Close behind the shell-hole stood a great, gaunt crucifix—the Christ hanging pale and vivid in the moonlight. With an effort he stood up, and saluted. He noticed that it was untouched by shells; one of the many wayside shrines that had escaped. Something struck him about the Figure. The half-closed eyes of the Crucified seemed to be looking down into the shell-hole at the man who was lying there—at the man who was His enemy. He stood, spell-bound by what he saw in that moonlit Christ stretched there amidst the terrors of the ridge. For it had come to him that Someone had suffered immeasurably more than himself—yes, infinitely more—for that mocking unbeliever below. He went and laid his blood-stained head against the wounded Feet. . . .

"Hullo there! Do you want to get cut off?"

He turned round with a start to see a limber-cart drawn up on the road. He called back loudly. Someone was springing down—running across to him. He went forward.

"Spotted you from the road. What's up?" The voice was familiar; and, as its owner came close, he recognized him for an officer of their own infantry.

"Why, it's not——? Yes, it is! Doc, what *are* you doing here?"

He pointed down the shell-hole. "Help me get him back, will you?"

The other took in the situation at a glance, and shouted to the driver of the limber-cart, who jumped down and hurried over to them.

"Go and talk to the horses, Doc, will you? We've just come through Hades. We'll bring him along; you're done in.—Here, have a pull at this!"

Five minutes later they were going down the road at a gallop, the Captain propped up against them on the floor of the cart. Half-an-hour, and they were at the dressing-station. The orderlies on duty carried the Captain inside. An M.O. came and looked at him. He was then taken, still unconscious, into the examining room.

As the infantry officer clambered back on to the limber-cart he said to him:

"Thank you for the good turn. Will you do me another?"

"What's that?"

"Forget about finding me with him up there."

The other had been guessing things on the way back. He understood. There was an immense admiration in his eyes as he replied:

"If you really want me to, yes. But, Doc—— Oh, Doc, you're great! . . . Cheerio!"

And the limber-cart passed into the night.

He went back into the hut to have his own wounds attended to. The M.O. recognized him, commented on the mud and blood, but asked no questions. The Captain, he found, was to be taken down immediately to the C.C.S. His own case was not so serious—flesh-wounds and loss of blood; he would wait and go down in the morning.

When he reached the Clearing Station next day, he found it was not the one to which the Captain had been taken. On the whole he was glad. It saved explanations.

Four weeks later he had rejoined his battery—fit again. To his surprise the Major had guessed the truth about his disappearance. The man who had seen the Captain knocked-out had also seen himself riding off towards the ridge. He had informed the Major of both facts. The Major had also learnt of his arrival with the Captain at the dressing-station.

"Doc," he had challenged him, "look me in the face and say you didn't go and get him! You saved his life. You're blushing like a two-year old."

He had admitted it, but refused to give more than the barest outline of what he had gone through that night. Then he had bound the Major by a solemn promise to tell no one. The Major had given his promise very reluctantly.

The Captain, he learnt later, had recovered, to be stationed at home for the rest of the War. They had never met again until the night of the accident. And the other had forgotten him and had not found out. . . .

The clock in the tower struck midnight.

Brother Anselm started—to find himself staring into the night. He sighed. Memories slipped away into the past once more. He stood up slowly. Then he went out of his cell down the corridor and had a last look at the Cripple. He was sleeping peacefully.

Down at the hotel another man also looked out of his window into the night. It was the Atheist. He was thinking about the monk.

His eyes were gleaming with hatred.

CHAPTER XI

The Major Needs a Tonic

§ 1

"READ IT, and tell me what you think," said the Cripple, handing an opened letter to Brother Anselm.

It was some days later. No more had been seen of the Atheist at the monastery. According to the Optimist, who had been up once or twice, he had turned silent and unsociable. On one occasion there had been heated words between him and the Major. He had accused the latter of not supporting him against "the monk's insults," and the Major had replied frankly: "I saw no occasion to support you. Brother Anselm was not insulting you; he was telling you some home-truths." After this relations between them had been somewhat strained. The Pessimist also added fuel to the fire by reading some book on philosophy lent him by Brother Anselm. The Atheist had sneered at him for "coming under the monk's influence." The other had retorted: "If I am, then I prefer it to yours." The Optimist had related all this, adding: "He even objects to my coming up here—says he's sorry to notice me 'losing my intellectual independence.'"

Today the Cripple had received a letter from his people in England. It had come with the afternoon post. He had been reading it through in his favourite place, under the trees in the garden. Brother Anselm had just joined him after Choir-office—to be greeted with the above request.

"Do you want me to read it all?" said the monk. "Nothing private, I mean?"

"Only one or two things about—— Well yes, read it all."

Brother Anselm smoothed out the sheets. On the corners of each were stamped the family arms. He read it through, and then gave it back to the Cripple.

"May I have a little time to think it over?"

"Yes, rather! Sort of wants thinking over, doesn't it?"

The Cripple spoke lightly; but there was a dread at his heart. The letter concerned his future—the future that he knew he would have to face.

"Anyway," he added, "that's that! . . . The Major's coming to tea, isn't he? Before he arrives—er—I want to tell you something."

"Do. Get it off your chest." Brother Anselm spread himself on the grass.

The Cripple cleared his throat.

"Well, you know what you said that day about the crucible— being tested and all that. I've—I've sort of plunged right in now—into the crucible. It was that day up at the village, I think, in the church at Benediction. It began there. God suddenly became real to me—quite close. He was a real Person Who loved me. I can't describe it; but there it was. I told Him what a blackguard I was; all about the appalling things I'd done—my sins, especially the damned rotten way I'd cursed Him—I hardly dared think about that. I was almost afraid to tell Him—but then, of course, He knew. I think that crowd in the church made it easier, all those babies and dogs and people. There they were all bang in His presence, and He seemed to love it—and love them all. I could tell Him then—and how appallingly sorry I was——"

He cleared his throat again.

"——I told Him too that I was just *going* to accept what had happened to me, and not grouse—I mean complain—any longer. Then, you remember when that attack of pain came on, when you got me back to bed. I'd often noticed the crucifix hanging on the wall before, but it didn't mean much. It began to mean something then. As the pain got worse, I remembered what I'd read in that book you lent me, about sharing the Cross with Christ; so I asked—well, if I might. I can't quite explain how; but when I'd done it, although the pain was terrible, it was different. It was as if I'd given Him the pain. The pain was still there of course; but the weight of it, that crushing part, had gone. The awful part seemed upon Him, not me. . . . But what came to me—of course, you'd said it, I know—but it came with such terrific force that it was God, that it really was God Himself on the Cross. It seemed so terrible, and so—magnificent."

The Cripple paused.

"Yes?" said Brother Anselm. "Go on."

"I don't exactly know how to go on. . . . It's like this. I've found out God; and I know He is a God of love. I just know it. But—I feel there's more than this. I still feel vague about things. All those people in the church were so—definite in their way of setting about it. They knew exactly what to do. They'd got something more, I'm sure of it. I didn't belong to them somehow. . . . And you're just the same. You're different to me. You've got something more—and I can't quite make out what it is. You are—inside somewhere. When you're talking to me, I feel that I'm outside. I'm sorry I can't put it better, but——"

"You couldn't put it better," said Brother Anselm.

The Cripple moved himself towards the edge of the ambulance.

"You understand, then? Well, what is it—this sort of *outside* feeling?"

Brother Anselm decided to risk it.

"I know exactly what it is you feel, and I know why you feel it. But first tell me this. Have you any religious prejudices, commonly called?"

"None whatever. I'm supposed to be a Protestant, I think. My people are Protestants, I believe; though they don't go anywhere. Yes, I'm sure they are, because there was an awful row once—when some relation became a Catholic."

Brother Anselm sat up and roared with laughter, until the tears ran down his face.

"Forgive me. I really am sorry; but—— Oh dear!" He went off again. . . . "I'm terribly rude; but, you know, your test of Protestantism *is* a bit funny. Now, let's be serious." He wiped his cheeks. "You don't feel like that yourself about the Catholic Church?"

"Not a bit."

"Very well. Now about that 'outside feeling.' Answer me this. Is it a mere feeling of curiosity; or is it a feeling of wanting something more than you have already?"

"I think it's something more that I want; a sort of hankering that I can't get rid of."

"And something more that I have, which you have not?"

"Yes.—Yes it is."

"Shall I tell you what you want?"

"Yes, I wish you would."

Brother Anselm plunged.

"You want the Catholic Church. You could not have that 'outside feeling' otherwise. Every convert to the Catholic religion has it before he becomes a Catholic. The Catholic Church is God's kingdom. You are outside God's kingdom—outside your home. That feeling of yours is home-sickness——"

"Which is the Tradesman's entrance?" It was the Major's voice that broke in upon them. "No, don't mind me, don't take any notice of me; I'm only the guest. I'll go and talk to the cook."

Brother Anselm rose from the grass and went forward to meet him.

"Sorry I didn't see you coming. Next time you shall have a procession of monks to receive you. Dear old Major! How are you? . . . Now, can you two amuse yourselves while I get tea? . . . Don't play pranks with that perambulator, Major! . . . No, he doesn't want wheeling about—not peevish today. . . . No, don't stand at his head; he's not a horse. Sit at his feet. . . . No, not *on* his feet! And that's not a gun-carriage. . . . Get off it, you hippopotamus! . . . Now, sit down—on the chair." The Major was bounced into the chair.

"You ought to have been a sergeant-major, not a monk. You've burst my collar." This was a parting shot at Brother Anselm walking off. "Great lad, the Doc!" he remarked to the Cripple. He attended to his collar, and then settled himself in the chair. "I can't get over this *monk* business though. Thought monks a bit queer, myself—shutting themselves up and all that. Doesn't seem to have changed him. Knew he was an R.C. of course in the Army—religious enough. But a *monk*! Can't imagine him knuckling under here."

"Why don't you ask him how he does it?" said the Cripple.

§ 2

Brother Anselm arrived with the tea shortly, including a generous supply of bread and butter, honey and cakes.

"Great scrounge that!" said the Major, eyeing the feast. "Where did you pinch it? Still got your old Army ways? . . . I say, I want to ask you something. Er—how do you manage to knuckle under here?"

"What exactly do you mean?" said the monk.

"Well, obey the rules and all that?"

147

"Oh, I see. It's not so very difficult. We're here to obey rules."

"Are they strict—the rules?"

"Very strict."

"But I'd run amok in a week's time."

"Probably you would. But you're not a monk, and you're not a Catholic."

"That makes a difference?"

"Very much so. We start with a totally different idea to you. Obedience is natural, in a sense, to Catholics: we take it for granted in the Catholic Church. Authority involves obedience.—You started this, Major."

The Major played with his moustache.

"Bit—servile, isn't it, caving in like that?"

"Not in your sense," said Brother Anselm. "And not if we're 'caving in' to God's authority. It's God's authority in the Catholic Church. It doesn't matter whether it's people obeying their priests, or priests their bishops, or bishops the Pope, or monks their superiors; it's God they're all obeying. And they all know it. Remember you're English. The idea of submitting to authority in religious matters does of course seem servile to most Englishmen, because they don't even know what submitting to God means."

"Bit sweeping that, isn't it?" said the Major.

"I don't think so," replied Brother Anselm. "I'd go further. I don't think the ordinary Englishman even realizes that God is a Person to be submitted to. Is his attitude one of submission? Look at the position Almighty God occupies in England today! Many don't take the slightest notice of Him; they're not even on speaking terms with the Almighty; openly boast that they've no religion—think it sounds clever. Some of them don't object to the Almighty as long as He's kept in the background and doesn't interfere. Quite a lot can't distinguish between themselves and the Deity—these Theosophists and Christian Scientists and

Modernists too. The most priceless of all are those who consider the Almighty rather old-fashioned, and invent a non-Almighty instead—a finite God, who is doing his best, but we must give him a helping hand. You see, all these good people simply do not know Who God is or what He is—the omnipotent Creator of heaven and earth and themselves; a Person to be submitted to, not apologized for. Even the few who are still Protestants don't realize what being Almighty God means. It really comes to this: the non-Catholic attitude towards God is fundamentally different to the Catholic attitude.—Is this boring you, Major?"

"Not a bit of it. I like it—new to me. Didn't come up here to pick buttercups. Carry on, Doc."

"Shall I show you the difference then?" said Brother Anselm. He was deliberately talking for the benefit of the Cripple as much as the Major. He thought. . . .

"I'll show you *what* God is. That's the best way. I'll show you what we are too. . . . God is our Creator. We are His creatures. He brought us into existence out of nothing. There was no need for Him to create us, mind you; and, even when He did, He created us not for ourselves but for Himself. Not only that, but God of His own free-will keeps us in existence. We hang upon Him like a stone on a string. If He let go the string we should instantly fall out of existence back into the nothingness from which we came.—Do you follow me?"

"Quite."

"Now those are the simple facts of our existence; and, as rational beings, we are bound to acknowledge them, by giving to God the homage of our whole being which belongs to Him. Unconditional surrender. Unconditional submission. That is the first rational act of a human being. That is the Catholic attitude towards God—an attitude of utter self-abasement."

"Bit drastic, isn't it?" said the Major. "Sounds almost degrading. Makes a fellow feel a perfect worm."

"No, the Catholic attitude does not degrade. A man does not degrade himself by recognizing what God is and what he is. He acts in a rational manner."

The Major helped himself to honey, feeling slightly uncomfortable. He had a smack at a fly with the honey-spoon.

"Yes," he said. "I think I see now how you manage to knuckle under. Takes the stuffing out of a fellow, believing it like that."

Brother Anselm laughed.

"Well," said the Major, "every man for himself! Believe what you like—and stick to it."

"You Britisher!" said the monk.

"Why?"

"That's a typical Britisher's remark—'believe what you like.'"

"But I've a right to."

"You've no right whatever to believe what you like. You've *no* religious rights."

The Major stared open-mouthed at Brother Anselm. . . .

"Is that a joke?"

"No. It's a fact. It's what I've been saying, in another form. You're a creature, man. You've no *rights* with your Creator—let alone religious rights. Religion's to do with your Creator. The Britisher insists that he has a *right* to believe what he likes— about the Christian religion; a *right* to make up a religion of his own; a *right* to his own opinions on morals and conduct. He has no such rights. When did Christ ever say a man had a right to believe what he liked? He taught exactly the opposite. The Britisher's attitude towards the Christian religion is precisely what you would expect from his attitude towards God. It is an attitude of non-submission: he's not going to be *told* what to believe, he's not going to be *told* what to do. That is why he refuses to pass under a certain doorway—on whose lintel is inscribed the word 'Submission.'"

"Look here, Doc," said the Major, "I'm not green. I know what you're getting at."

"So do I," replied Brother Anselm. "And the fact that the Catholic Church demands submission ought to be sufficient in itself. What else would you expect? Isn't the Church that Christ put into this world to exercise the authority He gave her? *His* Church was to be heard, to be obeyed, to bind and loose, to lay down laws, to excommunicate, to be believed under pain of damnation. . . . My dear Major, if all that does not mean submission, then what on earth *does* it mean? Submission to the Catholic Church means submission to God. God Himself has written that word 'Submission' over the doorway of His Church."

The Major looked flabbergasted.

"*Do you mean to tell me*—do you really expect the *British nation* to submit to the Catholic Church?"

"If the British nation does *not*," replied the monk, "so much the worse for the British nation. It's very rapidly becoming a choice now of the Catholic Church or paganism."

"It's rapidly becoming a choice for me of a stiff tonic or total collapse," said the Major.

Brother Anselm stood up and began to collect the tea-things.

"Still got your Army ways? We've nothing very stiff. If a liqueur will pull you round——?"

"Don't press me! don't press me! . . . Still, one likes to be sociable——"

"I'll do another scrounge," said Brother Anselm.

The Major watched him disappear. He lit a cigarette, and then scrutinized the Cripple.

"Did he really mean that—that submission business? Was he serious?"

"I'm certain he was."

"Do you believe it yourself?"

"I'm beginning to think I do. As far as I can see, you're simply driven to the Catholic Church—if you want the real thing."

"But you're not——?" The Major stopped.

"Thinking about it?" The Cripple finished the sentence. "Yes, I am. I rather expect it is going to be the Catholic Church for me."

The Major gasped.

"Confession! Infallibility! Purgatory! . . . You'll have to swallow the lot!"

The Cripple smiled.

"I don't think that will be very difficult. Most Christians believe these things; why not myself? . . . Look here, Major"—the Cripple suddenly became very serious—"I want something to hang on to. I want to know what to believe. Protestants can't tell you; they simply argue about religion and all contradict each other. The Christian religion can't be like that really. If Christianity is merely a matter of opinions, I can't see what good it is to anybody, or why anybody should believe it.—A fat lot the Protestant religion means to you!—If that's Christianity, then Christianity's a darned poor sort of thing—afraid to speak out or offend anybody. Christianity *can't* be like that." The Cripple pushed his hair off his forehead. "Major, I've come bang up against the Catholic religion here—I've been watching it, and reading about it—and it's an utterly different kind of thing. It's real. It's got authority; it's perfectly certain of itself. It knows. It's not afraid of the world; it doesn't climb down and pander to you—it doesn't lick your boots. It challenges you; dares you to deny! It's a terrific thing! . . . And these Catholics love it—passionately; I've seen them at it. It's what Christianity would be. It's what those martyrs died for, I'm certain. . . ."

The Cripple wiped his lips. His pale face was flushed.

The Major pulled vigorously at his cigarette, embarrassed at the outburst.

"Well, as I said, every man for himself. Believe what you——"

"Major, if you say that again, you'll not get a single drop of this"—it was Brother Anselm with a bottle of liqueur—"Instead, you'll get bounced again."

The Major grabbed the white cloth off the table and brandished it on the end of his cane, in token of surrender. "No, no! not that! Another bounce would be the end of me! . . . Doc, oh Doc, would you have me depart this life—unliqueured, unhonoured and unsung?"

"And unhung?" added Brother Anselm.

Chapter XII

The Cripple Decides

IT WAS NOT until the following morning that Brother Anselm broached the matter of the letter to the Cripple.

After he had settled him as usual in the ambulance the monk wheeled him through the monastery grounds and out of the gates along the road. They were both rather silent and not quite at ease. They turned off down a lane sheltered from the heat by the cool green of the pines, and, further on, came to a halt.

Brother Anselm sat down on the grass bank at the side.

"I've been thinking over what your people say."

"Yes?"

"Shall I tell you candidly what I think?"

"Yes, please do"—anxiously.

"You know I'm very fond of you, don't you?"

The Cripple looked away. Brother Anselm controlled his voice with an effort.

"If it were a question of my own feelings only, I should ask you to stay on here at the monastery. I should love to look after you always; you know that without my telling you. But your people——well, they are your people, aren't they?—and they have to be considered. It is only natural that they should want you to go home; after all, you are their son. Your father evidently takes it for granted that you will go home; otherwise he would scarcely have secured this—er—male-nurse that he mentions, to look after you."

"Sort of keeper," said the Cripple, crushing down the pain at his heart. "Dear old dad! I know it's awfully good of him; but, oh dear! Sounds rather like an asylum."

"I don't think there will be much difficulty there," said the monk. "You'll get used to the situation. After all, you've managed to get used to me."

"Yes, but you're *you*. And it's all part of your religion to—I mean you do it for the love of God. It makes it all so different. My helplessness doesn't seem humiliating when it's you looking after this old wreck. You do it as if it was a privilege; and I'm not fit to lick your boots." The Cripple swallowed. He thought for a little, and then said: "Do you think I ought to go home?"

"Yes, I do. Your father and mother want it; also, under the circumstances, I think your natural place is at home."

"Oh, you're right; I know you're right. But it's so horrible— the idea of leaving you, and all this. I can carry on fairly easily here; but at home, you see, there's no religion there."

The Cripple had often talked about his home. Brother Anselm had no difficulty in picturing the life there—a family to whom the world meant everything, with a reputation of being the smartest in the county; abundance of money, ceaseless entertaining of a loose hunting set. . . .

"No, I suppose not, from what you've told me," he said in answer. "That's the funny thing! Your father seems indifferent to religion himself, yet he obviously fears your staying on here in a monastery. His remark about your last letter having 'an unpleasantly Roman Catholic tone' is more what one would expect of a zealous Protestant. He hopes 'the kindness of this Brother Anselm is not influencing' you. I suppose he is afraid——"

"He's afraid of my becoming a Catholic!" burst out the Cripple. "And there'll be an awful row if I do. In fact, there *will* be an awful row, because——" He hesitated, half-fearing to say it. "Because I am going to be a Catholic."

The Cripple found those grey eyes looking into him. . . .

"In ninety-nine cases out of a hundred," said Brother Anselm, "if a person had come to an abrupt decision on the matter like that, I should have put it down to mere emotion, and told him to go on thinking and praying about it for some time longer."

The Cripple felt as if the whole interior of him were being inspected.

"With you though I don't think it is mere emotion. I answered your question yesterday as I did, because I was certain that God was opening your eyes to the truth, and because I knew you had surrendered your will. Conviction comes very quickly once a man surrenders everything to God."

The Cripple's eyes were shining. "Oh, I see it so clearly; as clearly as I see you sitting on that bank. Why—why doesn't everybody see it like this?"

"Because their eyes are blinded."

"But why? Why can't they find out?"

"I'm afraid the world sees to it, as far as possible, that they shall *not* find out. The world hates the truth. The masses in England are kept in perpetual prejudice and ignorance of the Catholic Faith by the lies and misrepresentations of its enemies—one long campaign of dust-throwing to blind them. Even the Press to a large extent assists the world. It almost invariably supports Modernism—that lie of lies, the very antithesis of the Faith of Christ."

"That man Inge's a Modernist, isn't he? Why does he hate the Catholic Church like that?"

"It's not my business to judge Dean Inge," said Brother Anselm. "I only hope he is one of those who 'know not what they do.' I only hope he is a blind leader of the blind. However——"

The monk paused. He wanted to make quite sure that the Cripple understood what becoming a Catholic meant. "Of course there are thousands who do see the truth and become Catholics, and there are thousands more who would do so if only they would give up things for God. That's the Englishman's curse. He's been accustomed to a religion that costs nothing. To become a Catholic costs something—the surrender of your intellectual pride, your self-love, your sins, your friends sometimes. You may lose by it—the things of the world; and so few are prepared to do it—to sacrifice themselves for God. But I am afraid that is the entrance-price of the Kingdom of Heaven."

The monk half expected a protest of self-sacrifice. He was glad when it did not come. The Cripple evidently took it for granted; for he remarked instead:

"Do you know the Major could scarcely believe you were serious yesterday in what you said about the Catholic Church—the submission idea?"

"Dear old Major!" said Brother Anselm. "He is a typical Britisher. I suppose it would seem a sort of intellectual suicide to him, submitting to an infallible authority."

"He practically said so. He couldn't imagine me swallowing Infallibility!"

"And I daresay he hasn't the faintest notion what it means," smiled the monk. "The comical thing is that so few people have—and yet get purple in the face over it. As if the Church could be anything else but infallible! Infallibility is the only guarantee that the Christian religion is true. The Church that teaches the truth *must* be infallible: truth is an infallible thing. If Christianity is not infallibly true, then there is no obligation upon any man to believe it. What's the good of getting up on your hind legs to tell people you don't know what the Christian religion is, or whether it's true—that's what it means if you're not infallible. The Major of course thinks it means *blind* submission. There's nothing blind about it. The Catholic Church comes to men open-handed: 'Here are my credentials, examine them; use your reason, examine my claims for yourself!' She comes with compelling claims, with overwhelming proofs, with the beauty of God shining in her eyes. Many men see her beauty and feel its lure; but they turn away when they see that word 'Submission' inscribed above her doorway. They try and forget that they have looked into their mother's eyes."

The Cripple became pensive.

"I'll have to risk the row with my people. I'll have to write and tell them—now."

"You would be wiser to wait a few days," said Brother Anselm. "I don't doubt your conviction, but I think you ought to give it a little longer test. In any case I could not receive you into the Catholic Church for some time yet; you would have to go through the ordinary course of instruction in the Faith first. Now, let me see. . . . Your father suggests the autumn for your journey to England—say two months from now. I could begin instructing you straight away. Under the circumstances, providing of course your conviction perseveres, I think we might receive you into the Church before you go back. When you write, I should tell your people quite openly that it is a matter of conviction and of conscience with you. Shall that be the programme?"

"Yes," said the Cripple.

They were silent on the way back, as they were often silent now. They understood each other. And Brother Anselm understood something then—that the Cripple would go home, at whatever cost, without a murmur.

The same day, in the afternoon, an unexpected visitor arrived at the monastery.

The Cripple Decides

The Cripple was reading in the garden, absorbed. So much so that he did not become aware of the rustling of feet over the grass until the owners of the same discovered their presence by laughing. He started, and looked up to find Brother Anselm standing there with a little person at his side. This little person ran forward gleefully and presented him with a paper bag of something.

"Innocente! . . . where *have* you blown from?"

He remembered her at once—the little peasant-girl of the village in the mountains. She stood by expectantly, watching for him to open the bag. He understood that was the first thing to do; so untwisted the ends and looked inside. The contents proved to be a sticky conglomeration of large, bright-coloured sweets.

"I say, how topping!" He successfully concealed his alarm at the prospect of eating them. "Are they really all for me? Let's have one each—first round."

For a minute or two the peace of the summer afternoon was disturbed by three sets of molars crunching at rock-like substances, which presently became reduced to the consistency of very firm glue threatening to remove the teeth from their sockets. Innocente won, more accustomed to the business; the Cripple came in second, and Brother Anselm made a bad third, finishing with a series of frantic gulps.

"Now tell me all about it," said the Cripple. "I want to know where Innocente has sprung from."

Brother Anselm acted as interpreter when necessary, the Cripple following the Italian child as best he could. It appeared that her father had taken her down in the cart to the town in the valley for market-day, and he had given her six soldi to spend, and Innocente had seen some most beautiful sweets on one of the stalls in the market-place, and she had given her six soldi to the woman, and the woman had given her a lot of the beautiful sweets, and Innocente had gone into the church, and she had remembered the signore in the "bed," because she always asked the Bambino Gesu in church to make him better, and she had told Gesu that she was going to give the signore the sweets because he was in "bed" and could not go to the woman in the market for sweets, and she had told father when they came out, and father had stopped at the monastery, and he was outside with the horse, and——

"And you are the most wonderful little person in the world!" said the Cripple impulsively, reaching out for her hand. There was a lump in his throat. He looked into Innocente's eyes— deep wells of perfect purity, wondering at the child's love for him shining there in the clear depths. This mite of seven loved him—because he was a cripple. She was lovely as a little Madonna, with those dark eyes and the olive-white complexion.

Then she told him all about her father and her mother and her brothers and her sisters and the cow and the pigs and her doll. His Italian vocabulary was decidedly limited, but with Brother Anselm's aid a fairly creditable conversation was achieved.

"Look here, we're forgetting father," the monk reminded them. "Come along, young lady!"

Innocente wanted the Cripple to come too. She would push the "bed." Brother Anselm thought perhaps they had better push it together. Beyond occasionally getting mixed up with Brother Anselm's legs, Innocente did her share nobly, inform- ing the Cripple, from somewhere underneath, that she pushed her doll about like this.

The father was waiting at the gates, hat in hand. After greeting the signore and hoping he had not minded the bam- bina coming to see him, he talked to Brother Anselm and then told Innocente they must start back. She kissed the Cripple good-bye and said she was coming to see him again and bring him more sweets. Brother Anselm lifted her into the cart and they drove off, Innocente waving until they disappeared round the corner.

Chapter XIII

The Atheist Knows

THERE WAS no doubt about it. His people had taken it very badly. He had written to them a few days after his talk with Brother Anselm, and now the reply had come. "... Your mother and I are pained beyond words. ... I am amazed at the effrontery of this monk. To ensnare you into the Catholic Church is disgraceful in any case; but to take advantage of your helpless condition is beneath contempt. ... I consider the step you contemplate taking an insult to the honour of your family. The Catholic religion may be all very well for the lower orders and foreigners, but . . ."

There were four pages of this kind of thing. His father seemed to take it as a personal injury. The Cripple's own conviction and conscience in the matter were ignored.

He asked Brother Anselm to read the letter. The monk did so, and then said quite simply: "Pray for them both. At present your father refuses to see that it is a matter of conscience with you. He wants to believe that you have been unduly influenced; he is not going to have it that it comes from yourself. His threat to write to the *Times* and expose me is—well, that's to stop me receiving you into the Church. I'm sorry he's taken it like this; I'm afraid it will make going home not quite so easy."

Brother Anselm did not tell the other what he read between the lines—the selfish pride of an irreligious man whose conscience had been stung by his son taking religion seriously.

162

He noticed that the Cripple, though rather sad, had taken it quite calmly. Things like this seemed to matter little to him now. There were other signs too to tell the monk how rapidly he was advancing—the man who, not so long ago, had cursed God! Since the Benediction in the village the Cripple had asked every day to be taken into the monastery church. He would lie there very quiet facing the Tabernacle on the altar. The inward peace of his soul was manifesting itself in his very bearing. The singular beauty of his face struck Brother Anselm very forcibly at this moment.

"You are being plunged very deep in the crucible," he said. "It is not often God asks so much. He is asking everything from you."

Yes, thought the monk, everything. His body had been broken; the pleasures of life taken away. There was the complete helplessness, the humiliating dependence on others, the terrible anguish of those times of pain. And now there had come upon him the bitterness and anger of his own people.

"And soon He will ask me for you," said the Cripple with a sad smile.

Brother Anselm took his hand.

"I am only a prop. You will carry on now. You are on the road to Calvary. It is the way He makes His saints."

The Cripple kissed the big, rough hand that held his own, as he had once seen the children in the village do.

Meanwhile the stay of the party at the hotel was drawing to a close. The Major and the other three were leaving for England in two days' time.

Brother Anselm had invited them to meet the Cripple and himself up at the village in the mountains on the day of the conversation just recorded. The rendezvous was to be the caffè terrace after Benediction in the afternoon. It was to be a kind of farewell gathering. He had left it to the Major to ask the Atheist or not, as he thought best. The Major decided not to do so, the man's antagonism towards the monk was still so marked that no good could come of them meeting again. As it happened the Atheist announced his intention in the morning of making a visit by car to one or two places; he would not be back until dinner in the evening. The Major congratulated himself on the way being cleared so easily; there was no need now even to mention the meeting at the caffè. Unfortunately it never occurred to him to ask the Atheist which places he intended to visit.

And so it was that the unforeseen thing happened.

The coffee-and-cakes part was over. The proprietor of the caffè had placed wine upon the table, waiting upon the signori himself. Not every day did a party of Englishmen patronize his terrace.

They were all in a happy mood, in spite of the approaching farewell. The bracing air of the mountains, the view, the good wine and all had an exhilarating effect. Even the Pessimist was laughing at the Major's funny stories—told in his comic, jerky way. The Cripple, as usual, was chaffing the Optimist. . . .

"Keep quiet, you two," called Brother Anselm. "The Major's got a funny story."

"Weren't the others funny?" said the Cripple. "Go on, Major."

The Major cleared his throat.

"It was a drawing-room party I was at——"

"Who let you in?" asked the Cripple.

"——it was a drawing-room party I was at. Somebody started competition games, and offered a prize to the person who could make the funniest face. Loud applause. The guests sat round—features screwed up into every conceivable kind of grimace. I was appointed judge, and I went round examining each face in turn. Finally I approached an elderly lady who appeared to be making a remarkably funny face. 'Madam,' I said, 'I award you the prize.' The lady replied in icy tones: 'Sir, I am not playing.' I shall never forget the sensation it——"

"You awful man!" cried the Cripple. "You *awful* man! That one was in *Punch*—years ago."

"Eh?... Was it now? Was it really? I must have mixed it up—— Oh well, it was a drawing-room party—— Look here, how on earth can a fellow tell stories——"

He gave it up and joined in the convulsions of laughter.

"Giving a fellow away——"

The Major suddenly stopped. The merriment died out of his face, a heavy frown taking its place. He was staring fixedly at something. The others followed the direction of his eyes; and received a shock too. A car had drawn up at the entrance to the terrace, and someone was getting out.

It was the Atheist.

He walked in through the gates and strolled across to the parapet, standing there to take in the view. He had not noticed them yet; they were in the further corner. There was a minute of suspense, and then he turned round—and saw them.

It was an embarrassing moment.

The Atheist, after the first surprise, recovered himself quickly. But he had grasped the situation in a flash. He had been deliberately left out of all this. It was the monk's doing. ... His hatred surged up. He was too clever a man to let them notice anything, however. He would not make a fool of himself a second time. He advanced. ...

The Major decided to make the best of it.

"So you've found us, have you? How's the car going?"

"Splendid, thanks. I ought to have said this morning that I was stopping here on the way back. I thought I'd see the view. I must say it's marvellous—not a bit overrated."

The others breathed more easily. He was taking it nicely after all.

"Have a drink?" said the Major.

"Thanks. Dusty work on the roads."

The Atheist sat down and lit a cigarette, to all appearances completely at his ease. He had taken no notice of Brother Anselm so far. They were sitting some distance apart, the others between them. He talked about his drive in the car and the places he had seen, and then launched on to general subjects. He could talk well when he chose. He was obviously choosing to do so now.

Brother Anselm watched him. Why had he stayed? He could quite easily have made some excuse for continuing his journey. The monk's intuition told him there was some scheme working in that busy brain; the Atheist was playing for time. He was talking for a purpose; he was setting himself to gain the interest and sympathy of the others.

They were listening now to his opinions on certain political questions. Brother Anselm began to understand the man's peculiar power—that power he had exercised for a time over the Cripple. There was a compelling fascination about him—like this.

They had entered upon the subject of the War, the sacrifice of life involved, and finally, for some reason or other, the dishonour of those who refused to hear their country's call. . . .

Then Brother Anselm began to see. Without appearing to do so the Atheist was deliberately steering the conversation. Towards what? . . .

"Those who went through the War——"

The Atheist paused, and then repeated louder:

"Those who went through it all were filled with just contempt for the cowards who refused to serve in such a cause until practically compelled to do so. It is scarcely conceivable that there were Englishmen so lost to all sense of shame as to proffer any excuse to save their skins. Unfortunately they managed to make their excuses sound so plausible as to conceal the fact that they were despicable shirkers. Don't you agree with me, Major?"

"There were some, I've no doubt," replied the Major, wondering why the Atheist was emphasizing the point so. His remarks seemed forced—and unnecessary, considering that they had all served in the War.

"There were even those who sheltered themselves behind religion," continued the other, "claiming exemption on the ground of their religious duties. These skulkers should have been combed out like the rest—men who professed to serve the highest interests of humanity, and when it came to the test, hid themselves away in the hour of humanity's need. They may have congratulated themselves; but they lost the respect of all who did their bit out there."

"I don't quite know whom you are referring to," said the Major, "but there were priests enough at the front. I had the greatest respect for their work. I know for a fact that they gave their lives again and again in the course of their duties. Anyway—— What do you think is behind this business in China?"

"I am not alluding to the ones who were out there," said the other, refusing to be put off. "I am alluding to those who were not. What were the Religious Orders doing?"

"Sending out their priests too," quickly answered the Major. "Some had to stay behind, I take it, to carry on the ordinary jobs."

The Atheist hesitated for a moment—feeling his way. The others were looking bewildered, unable to perceive what he was driving at. Then it came:

"Those who stayed behind, shut up in their monasteries, forfeited all right to talk about a God of love. Those of us who went through that hell are the ones to judge——"

"May I suggest," said Brother Anselm, "that instead of addressing your remarks *at* me, you address them *to* me."

The Atheist had been waiting for this. He had struck home at last. He was on sure ground now. The monk, he had guessed, had not served in the War. He had never alluded to it. Not only this, but his continued silence under the deliberately provoking remarks spoke louder than any words. The challenge of course was mere bravado. It contained the monk's virtual admittance that he had stayed behind. The Major knew it and was shielding him.

"Certainly," he answered confidently, "if you wish it; though I should have thought you would have preferred not to draw attention to yourself—under the circumstances."

The Major started. It had come to him in a flash that he had never told the other even that Brother Anselm had been in the army.

"Certainly," repeated the Atheist. "I will do as you wish. You had the impertinence to address your insulting remarks to me the other——"

"Look here, chuck it!" interposed the Major. "It was a different matter then. He caught you at an underhanded game, and told you exactly what he thought of——"

"And *I* am going to tell *him* exactly what I think of him. There's no occasion for you to interfere, Major." He turned to the monk. "My opinion of you is my opinion of all monks who hid themselves away instead of taking their place at the front. You were a cowardly pack of shirkers! . . . I suppose it was the will of your God that you should keep out of it! I always thought religion was a soft sort of thing."

Brother Anselm said nothing.

His silence was perplexing the others to the verge of exasperation. The Cripple had been about to interrupt; but a warning glance from the monk had checked him—and the others too. They were all on the point of breaking in. Why didn't he speak—say that he had been through the War? He was making no attempt to defend himself. Instead he was gazing calmly at the view in front.

"You are not merely shirkers, you are hypocrites too, you people!" The Atheist was determined to lash the monk out of what he thought was an assumed indifference to conceal his chagrin. "The other day you preached at me; you dared to vaunt your pretensions of serving others for the love of God. You do it! You had chance enough in the War. Why didn't you come out there and do things for the love of God? The religion of you monks is what I always thought it—a canting, selfish sham; white-washed hypocrisy!"

Brother Anselm remained impassive.

"The love of God! There is *no such thing* as the love of God. Religion is so much snivelling self-interest, when it's put to the test of——"

"Damn it all! I *must* speak . . . I *must*," the Major burst out. He could hold himself in no longer. He looked appealingly at the monk.

Brother Anselm slowly rose. . . .

"I must go and settle up at the caffè."

He was coming to some decision.

"Yes, Major, you may speak now." Then he bent down and said in an undertone: "And—I release you from that promise."

He walked across the terrace and passed through the entrance into the caffè.

The Atheist was watching the Major. There was a sudden fear behind his defiant expression; the monk's abrupt disappearance had completely baffled him. The others were in a state of tension.

The Major moved his chair so as to face him squarely. He drew a deep breath. . . .

"So you called him a cowardly shirker! A cowardly shirker! . . ." He said each word slowly. "You were hoping your slanders would turn us against him.—Yes, I said 'slanders.' You knew in any case that Brother Anselm was not what you called him. Do you imagine we should think one shade the less of him even if he had never been out there?—Yes, I said 'even if he had never been out there.' Cowardly shirkers don't do what he's done for——" He looked towards the ambulance. "Even if he had been shut up in the monastery—well, that's his job, not yours. As it happens though, he was not. Make sure of your target; you got a bit wide of it this time. I'm going to tell you something. Brother Anselm was not a monk during the War; he was still practising as a doctor. He served in the British Army as M.O. He was with the gunners—attached to a certain battery. And that battery was mine. . . ."

The Atheist looked as if he had been struck. Defiance gave place to stupefaction. He parried.

"I—I don't believe it. I was in your battery. I—I should have remembered him."

"Yes, you *should* have. A pity you did not! You were with us for a few weeks. It was long enough for him to remember you; and short enough for you to forget him, it seems. He knew you, my friend, when he saw you again. You see, it was rather unlikely that he would forget you."

The Major looked round at the others, as if to prepare them for something—and then back at the Atheist.

"Would you like to know why? Do you remember asking me a certain question, and I told you I couldn't answer it because I was bound by a promise not to?"

The other suddenly sat up rigid, his mouth open.

"I have just been released from that promise," said the Major.

He bent forward.

"You asked me who saved your life at the front. . . . It was Brother Anselm who saved your life."

The Major folded his arms and sat back.

It had come as a thunderbolt—well-nigh electrifying every man of them. The dénouement was so abrupt that the others remained speechless, scarcely able to credit what they heard,

"And you called him a cowardly shirker!"

"I—I don't bel——"

The words died on his lips. It was useless. The Major's statement was that of a man who knew the truth of what he was saying. The Atheist recognized it—the play of his face revealing his reluctance to do so. He had gone deadly white. He made one more futile attempt to refuse the unpalatable fact. Then his body relaxed, and he sat there with his shoulders drooping as under the effects of a blow.

"It may not be convenient to believe it—that's what you mean. I daresay not. And please don't imagine Brother Anselm told me this himself—of his own accord. It may interest you to learn that I guessed it, before I got it out of him. When I find that you are left behind at night amongst the corpses on a hell-spot—you remember that ridge well enough, that wipe-out—and when I find that a man is seen going back to that hell-spot, and when I find that two hours later the same man reaches the dressing-station with you in a state of delirium and himself pretty well knocked-out—when I find out things like that, I begin to guess. And when I discover one or two other little things—like his starting on a horse and coming back without one, and shell-splinters being taken out of him, and four weeks at a C.C.S.—when I discover things like this, I come to the conclusion that this 'cowardly shirker' not merely saved your life, but went through hell to do it."

The Atheist was breathing heavily. He shifted his position.

"Four weeks after that night the Doc turned up from the C.C.S., the marks of what he'd been through still upon him. I challenged him to deny what I knew he had done—gone and got you back. He admitted it, but bound me by promise not to tell a living soul. I could get very little out of him; he refused to talk about it. But I know this much; what he did would have been mighty difficult for most of us. There's something somewhere, isn't there, about loving your enemies? Not an easy thing to do. But if ever it was done—well, I reckon it was done that night——"

He stopped. He had caught sight of Brother Anselm returning. The others saw him too.

As he came near, they stood up—spontaneously.

"No, no—please," said Brother Anselm. It seemed to distress him. They sat down again. He put away the Cripple's hand, held out to him. This kind of thing was obviously painful. He was not thinking of himself. All his thoughts were on the Atheist. He had not risen with the others, but remained in his chair. And he remained there now, his head down, waiting. . . .

Brother Anselm stood with his arms folded, looking down upon the man who had vilified him. The Cripple was leaning forward from his ambulance, his eyes shining with unashamed admiration. Opposite, on the other side, sat the Major upright, gnawing impatiently at his moustache, obviously hoping to see that slanderer receive his due. The two others, also upright, were wondering why the monk was looking at him like that.

The cry of a bird was borne up from the gulf in the rocks beneath. No other sound broke in upon the group waiting there on the terrace—waiting for the lash to descend.

But no lash came.

Instead, a great longing crept into the monk's look. There was no need for him to ask what the Major had said. It was written there in every line of that defeated figure.

He knew now.

When at last Brother Anselm spoke, his voice was full of pity.

"I am sorry for you. I let him tell you because—well, you said that our religion was a selfish thing—self-interest. You said that there was no such thing as the love of God. . . . Do you know why I did it?"

Silence. The Atheist was staring in front of him, not looking at the monk.

"I did it for the love of God. I don't think there was very much self-interest in it; there hardly could have been under the circumstances. You see, I could not leave you to die there, knowing you for what you were—your life and all. I hope you don't mind my saying this; but, if I had not loved God enough to do it, I don't know that I could have done it at all. Can you bring yourself to believe that; that it *was* done for the love of God?"

Silence.

"When we do things that are not easy, we do them for God. It is part of our religion. You are here today—you owe your life to our religion. Won't you think a little more gently of——?"

Brother Anselm did not finish the sentence. The Atheist had raised his eyes and met his own. It was only for a moment. Then he stared again in front of him with eyes narrowing into black slits, his mouth set in a hard straight line. He was repressing, refusing, driving down something fiercely—something that was striving for the upper hand. . . .

The monk shivered.

An intangible fear passed over him, a horror of some terrible thing. Unconsciously he moved away slightly, as from an evil presence. His heart was sinking with dread. He could say nothing more to that rigid, impenetrable figure.

The Angelus bell broke in upon them from the village church.

Brother Anselm crossed himself, repeating the words in a whisper. The dread left him. That bell, however, and the monk's prayer had another effect on the Atheist—an effect so malevolent that even the Major shrank back amazed. Some raging malignity had surged up, distorting the hard set of his face into an expression of fiendish malice.

"For God's sake, man, don't!" burst out the monk. "For God's sake! . . . Are you mad? Are you going to damn your soul to hell?"

"*Hell?*"—echoed back from the cliffs.

The Atheist stood up.

He stared insolently at the monk. He moved away, pushed back his chair—and stared again. An ugly, mocking peal of laughter broke from his lips. . . .

And then, without a word, he left them.

Chapter XIV

The Cripple Tested

§1

IT WAS AUTUMN.

Two months had passed, all too quickly for the Cripple. A week more, and he would be making his journey to England. The Major and the others had said farewell two days after the affair at the caffè. The dramatic culmination of matters between Brother Anselm and the Atheist had relieved them of the latter's company; for on their return to the hotel afterwards, it was found that the Atheist had already left—evidently wishing to avoid them. He was not seen again.

He had vanished from their lives.

The Major had written from London later on to say that he would like to superintend the Cripple's journey himself—he was "used to transport work." He would come back a week before the date fixed. That morning he had arrived, to be duly ensconced in one of the monastery guest-rooms, Brother Anselm having refused to hear of him stopping at the hotel. Two male nurses—"keepers" the Cripple called them—were following.

The Cripple was now a Catholic. He had been received into the Church by Brother Anselm the previous morning, and had made his first Communion immediately afterwards. That ineffable experience coupled with the sacramental absolution preceding it had left him quite bewildered by the love of God—the God Whom four months ago he had cursed! Who had saved him from suicide by the almost miraculous intervention of His monk.

He lay there now in the garden he had learned to love so well; his garden of peace. He had watched its trees clothing themselves with the full green of summer and then mellowing into the golden yellow of their autumn glow. Today the garden seemed very wonderful—a garden of God. His very breath stirred the leaves and rustled in the tree-tops; His voice was in the tinkling stream and in the song of birds; every sunbeam was gilded with His glory. The very leaves were falling at His touch.

But God was not merely without and about him now. He was present to him, in his soul, in his innermost being. That was what the Catholic Church had done—placed him in personal relationship with a Person. She had given him a direct spiritual experience of God. His submission to the Church had proved to be as Brother Anselm had said, submission to God. He had become as a child and entered the Kingdom of Heaven. He was in the arms of a mighty Mother, whose strength was the strength of God. His very life pulsed through the veins of her body. At the touch of her fingers Divine graces poured into his soul. And his whole impulsive, generous nature was responding to the God of love as harp-strings to the human hand.

And so there was music in his soul and gladness in his eyes as he lay there in the garden that autumn day amidst the falling leaves. Leaves of brown, yellow leaves, leaves tinged with red—he watched them zig-zagging downwards until they rested with a sigh upon the earth, wondering what the garden would look like when all the trees were bared. To his quickened imagination this slow stripping of the trees seemed symbolical of his own life. He was being slowly stripped of everything. It would be Brother Anselm next. He hardly dared to think of that. For he loved that great rough, masterful man who had cared for him like a mother; who sacrificed himself for others and hated it to be known. He would never forget him apologizing for letting the Major tell them what he had done—"I'm sorry, my dears. I don't think I've ever hated myself so much. I did it because I thought it might change him, if he knew. And—and I've failed." And then before them all he had buried his head in his arms, and cried his big heart out for the soul he had tried to save.

There was little Innocente too. The child had woven herself into his life in a strange way. She had come to see him many times—every market-day in fact. He had polished up his Italian with Brother Anselm's aid, and their talks had progressed famously. Innocente knew now that he would always be "like that in bed." She had asked him one day when he would be able to "run about" with her, and he had explained why he would never be able to run about. She had been very unhappy about it until Brother Anselm told her that the Cripple was one of God's "chosen ones." Then she had looked almost enviously at him and asked Brother Anselm if she could be a "chosen one" too.

Today he would see her for the last time. She was coming to say good-bye.

§ 2

It was three o'clock; the hour at which Innocente generally arrived.

The Cripple was at the gates; Brother Anselm and the Major strolling up and down the gravel-drive near by. He had not long to wait before the market-cart came in sight, climbing slowly up the hill. Innocente saw him and waved. Her father raised his hat.

As the cart came near, he could see that she had brought the doll to say good-bye too, and a bunch of flowers—for himself he guessed. She was wearing her blue "market-frock." At the gates her father climbed out and lifted her down. The Cripple raised himself to prepare for the usual effusive greeting. But Innocente, instead of coming straight to him, ran across to the other side of the road. She had seen some flower on the bank and wanted to pick it. The father advanced and greeted him, as Brother Anselm and the Major came up.

It was at that moment that a car—a large touring-car—came round the corner unnoticed by them, running swiftly and silently down the hill.

And then the thing happened. . . .

It happened with a terrible suddenness. It happened before their eyes. For, as the car came level with the gates, its whirr caused them to look towards the road. Innocente was skipping across, holding up her bunch of flowers for the Cripple to see. The driver of the car had his eye on the horse and cart, and did not notice her. He heard them shout. There was a screeching of brakes. . . .

It was too late. The car had caught that little dancing figure and flung it aside. . . . For a few seconds things seemed to stand still. A sickening sensation gripped the Cripple. He closed his eyes. . . .

He opened them slowly. Brother Anselm was across there. He was on one knee, bending over something—over a twisted little heap. The Major was there too, bending over, and the father with his hand over his eyes. He saw the Major look up sharply and say something to the driver of the car, who was waving his hands about and trying to explain. He kept quiet then. Next, the Major was taking off his coat. Brother Anselm took it and very slowly began to work it under what the Cripple now began to realize was Innocente's body.

When that was done, Brother Anselm lifted the burden in his arms. The Major stood aside to let him pass. He was coming through the gates. As he passed, the Cripple looked. He saw two little legs dangling in a helpless sort of way—no more. The father followed behind with his head down, his face drawn and haggard.

The Major stayed a moment to pick up the doll which was lying in the middle of the road, and collect the flowers scattered about. He hesitated, glanced towards the Cripple, and came across. Without meeting his eyes he laid the doll on the ambulance and put the flowers into his hand.

He started after the others. Something, however, occurred to him; for he came back, turned the ambulance round and wheeled the Cripple down the drive to the entrance of the monastery. Neither of them spoke.

The Major went inside.

The Cripple looked at the flowers. . . .

And then it was that the horror of what had happened broke upon him. Innocente had been—— No, it couldn't be that! He shuddered. He tried not to think. . . .

Then, all in a moment, a tempestuous fury was raging at his soul—striving to lash him to revolt; to deny; to hate! Snatches from the Atheist's arguments dinned in his ears. He felt his faith being torn at by unseen hands—derided by mocking lips. He clung on with his will. . . . "Oh, my God!—My God!" He fought it down. The fury abated. He became calm again.

One of the monks came out and walked quickly towards the gate, where the driver was pacing up and down. He spoke to him. The man went to his car, backed and turned, and drove away up the hill. He had gone to fetch the mother from the village in the mountains, the Cripple learnt later.

A long half-hour of suspense.

And then he heard footsteps inside and a latch clicking. The door opened and Brother Anselm came out. The Major and one of the other monks were with him, but stayed within the doorway.

Brother Anselm came to the Cripple. There was a dark stain all down his habit.

"You would rather I told you?"

"Y—es. Yes, tell me."

"She is conscious now; but she is dying. I don't think she can last very long; perhaps an hour or two. Would you like to be taken in—to be with her?"

"Yes—I want to," the Cripple replied hoarsely.

"She has received absolution and been anointed. I am going to give her Viaticum, if possible—now."

He added: "She knows nothing of what has happened. She wants to give you some flowers—and cannot find them. Let her see that you have them."

He spoke to the Major, and then went inside again with the other monk. The Major came and turned the ambulance, and wheeled the Cripple inside through the doorway, down the main corridor. He stopped at a door on the left and opened it. The Cripple noticed a smell of chemicals. He found himself inside a large room. A sense of stillness struck him. In the middle of the room there was a large table, at the further side of which a man, the father, was sitting. He looked up as they entered, his eyes returning almost immediately to their vigil. In a corner was a basin containing pieces of blue frock. The Major moved the ambulance alongside the table.

The Cripple looked.

In the centre, on a mattress and wrapped in a blanket, lay a small figure. The head was heavily bandaged. Beneath the bandaging a little white face appeared. The eyes were closed. The Cripple could hardly realize it was Innocente. The waxen pallor made her look different. She seemed far away. There was something about the arranging of the blanket which spoke of terrible injury. She was moaning now—and freeing her arm, as if trying to find something.

The father rose and came round the table. He took the child's hand gently and placed it in the Cripple's. Her eyelids flickered and opened. She looked about her and, as her eyes rested on him, a faint light came into them. He showed her the bunch of flowers.

The tinkling of a bell became audible. As the sound came nearer, the father knelt down. The door opened and a monk entered—then Brother Anselm carrying Something under a veil. The first monk lit two candles, placing them on a table at the side, and knelt down. The Major knelt down too—rather awkwardly. Brother Anselm was reciting some Latin words, the other monk responding. There were genuflections, and then they were bending over Innocente, the one holding a white cloth under her chin as Brother Anselm placed the Host on her tongue. They watched for a minute, then went back to the table at the side. The rite completed, Brother Anselm made the sign of the Cross with What he was holding under the veil. ... They were gone.

The tinkling of the bell died away in the distance, and stillness reigned once more. The room was different now to the Cripple. The stillness was full of a tremendous Presence— filled with a vast, overwhelming Love. The sharp sword of agony had been placed in its sheath. He became aware that the horror of it had gone, at the touch of a mighty Hand. It was as if Someone had taken that babe into His arms and said: "You may leave all the rest to Me."

Brother Anselm was back.

He drew a chair up to the table, sitting close. He was leaning over, whispering some words. The Cripple caught the Holy Name. She was repeating it after him faintly. Now he was holding a crucifix to her lips. He placed it where she could see it; then sprinkled Holy Water.

They watched in silence.

The moaning began again—and stopped rather suddenly. Her eyes opened, slowly and wearily. She was trying to say something. Brother Anselm bent over to catch the words. . . .

"She is 'very, very tired,'" he repeated to them.

He was listening again. . . . He looked up at the Cripple.

"When she sees God, she is going to tell Him about you."

The Cripple took the little hand in his own.

Brother Anselm began to recite some more prayers.

It was now that the Cripple understood what was happening in this room. He saw the table in the middle as a kind of altar on which Innocente was being offered. She had been asked of them; they were giving her back. The human anguish of it all was there, in his heart, in the tears that had brimmed over and were running down his cheeks—yes. But that anguish was almost swallowed up in the knowledge born of faith; that, if they loved Innocente, there was Someone Who loved her immeasurably more; Someone Whose everlasting arms were reaching down to take her to Himself; Someone Who had created her, to Whom she belonged, to Whom she was returning; Someone Who had agonized and offered Himself that she might be with Him eternally. That little figure in the blanket meant infinitely more to Him than it ever could to them. Eternal Love was waiting.

A change was coming.

She had lapsed now into unconsciousness. Brother Anselm's fingers were on her wrist. They could see a shadow stealing over. . . .

There was a pause.

Outside in the grounds a bird chirruped—the sound of it accentuated in that living silence. A great peace seemed to radiate from the centre, from where Innocente lay.

The western sun had crept round the trees of the garden. Rays of golden light were flooding into the room, beyond where the table stood.

Brother Anselm was on his knees as the breathing altered. The foremost ray had reached the table. . . . It was climbing slowly, over the bandages on the head. . . .

A long sigh came—the sigh of a tired child settling down to sleep. The golden glory was moving onwards . . . over the face . . . touching the mouth. . . .

The baby lips were parted in a kind of wondering smile.

She was dead.

Chapter XV

The Major is Mystified

T
HE CAT RUBBED round the Major's legs, by way of inviting him to continue that very pleasant tickling on the top of its head. The Major however did not respond this time.

He had been walking up and down in the dark on the path that ran alongside the monastery church, listening to the last chants of the monks' Vespers. A bell in the tower had boomed forth good-night over the garden and down into the valley. Once he had heard the door round the corner open, and shut; then the crunch of gravel, followed later by the sound of wheels on the road—the dead child's father and mother departing for the night. And the hush of the star-lit heavens had descended once more.

He had lighted a cigarette, the cat seizing her opportunity of securing his attentions. He was standing still now, unresponsive to the creature's wiles, wondering why the great windows above him still glowed faintly from some light within. He could hear nothing. There was no more singing. . . . He threw down his cigarette. The cat sprang aside from the sparks, and walked off—insulted.

There was a side door at the end of the path. He would discover whether it was still open. He had never seen the church inside. . . . Yes, the door gave at his push. He was within. A smell of stale incense greeted him.

His first impression was of a forest of pillars, soaring up-wards into darkness—bars of black interspaced with light from behind. The source of this light was concealed from his view. He crept clear of the shadows until the long length of the nave opened out.

Then he saw something which riveted his attention—something which was to impress itself indelibly on his memory. . . .

In the centre, at the further end of the nave facing the entrance to the choir, lay the Cripple in his ambulance—motion-less. As motionless as that which was before him. For beyond the ambulance stood a small coffin covered with a white pall. On either side there were candles burning, their dancing flames emphasizing the immobility around. Beyond the coffin again, and far above in the dimness, a great crucifix was hanging, the figure of the Christ caught by the candle-light from below. It was only his fancy perhaps, but from where the Major stood the Christ seemed to be looking directly down upon the Cripple and the coffin.

He was not an imaginative man; but, as he watched, the impression was borne upon him of some kind of relationship between these three. It may have been that the candle-light had grouped them together out of the surrounding darkness, merely associating them to his own sight. But certainly the impression was very vivid. It was almost as if there was a conver-sation going on between them. Yes—an intimate conversation.

The Major felt a little uncomfortable. He wondered whether he ought to be looking on. A sense almost of guilt came over him; of having stumbled upon something not meant to be seen.

There *was* something going on there. . . .

He looked towards the door at which he had entered, and began to creep away on tip-toe. Just before the pillars would have hidden the nave from sight he glanced back. He stopped.

Someone was coming out of the darkness down the choir into the circle of light. . . .

It was Brother Anselm. He was passing the coffin, and approaching the Cripple to speak to him.

The Major saw the monk stand still—and then draw back a little. He had apparently noticed something unusual. He was hesitating. He went up to the ambulance and touched the other on the shoulder. . . .

The Cripple did not move.

Brother Anselm touched him again. . . . Still he did not move.

The Major began to feel afraid. Had anything happened? He had better make his presence known. He turned back and walked cautiously up the nave. Half-way he paused. Brother Anselm was kneeling down, looking upwards at the crucifix.

The Major felt reassured, but rather at a loss; not quite liking to disturb the monk. He must wait. It was certainly very perplexing; but there could not be anything seriously wrong. Brother Anselm appeared to be taking whatever it was quite calmly.

It seemed rather out of place to be standing there staring. The Major, though not exactly a religious man, felt he ought to do something religious. He knelt down.

After a few minutes Brother Anselm rose, looked once more at the Cripple, and then came down the nave to where the Major was kneeling. He showed no surprise at seeing him. He must have known all the time that he was there. The Major stood up. Brother Anselm smiled. He was wiping his cheeks; they were all wet. He led him to the door.

Outside, the Major burst out:

"What's the matter? Why's he like that? Looks queer to me!"

Brother Anselm linked arms without answering and walked him up and down in the dark. Then he halted, facing him, and put both hands on his shoulders.

The Major is Mystified

"Dear old Major! It's rather difficult to explain. If you were a Catholic it would be different. I mean, you would understand then."

The Major looked perplexed.

"But is he all right?"

"Yes, quite. The good God is looking after him. He is—— Well, it's a way God has with His chosen ones." Brother Anselm knew it would be no good telling him what was really happening to the Cripple.

The Major looked more mystified than ever.

"Darned queer thing—your religion!"

"Never mind," said the monk. "You see, Major, he is rather a wonderful person; although he doesn't know it. He is going to be a saint, I think. Everything is being taken from him—today Innocente. That is the way God makes His saints; by taking everything from them. He loved that little child; but he never questioned, in spite of what it cost. He loves God more. Do you know what he said to me after it was all over?——"

The Major shook his head, without speaking.

"——'I wanted to give something—so I've given Him Innocente. Don't you think she's rather a beautiful gift?'"

Brother Anselm moved towards the door as he added: "We made that little coffin so that she could be in the church tonight. When everything was finished he asked where she would be. I told him—under the crucifix. He asked if he could be there with her. That is why he is there now. I must go back."

He opened the door and went inside.

The Major blew his nose. . . .

A pair of gleaming eyeballs appeared from out of the darkness. Their owner began to squirm round his legs.

"Hullo, cat; so you've turned up again!"

The cat found herself picked up. She began to purr—doubtfully at first, and then louder. Perhaps he had not thrown that cigarette at her after all. . . . Suddenly she found herself returned to the ground.

"Damn it all! . . ."

The Major blew his nose again.

The following has been pieced together from a letter written by Brother Anselm to a priest in England, into whose care he was committing the Cripple.

It appears that the Cripple remained in his motionless state for about half an hour; also that during this period he was entirely insensible to outer things. The monk remarks on "the peaceful intentness of his face, touched with a peculiar radiancy." Elsewhere he says: "When he came to himself again, it was as if he were awakening from sleep. Beyond being a little confused and absent-minded, he seemed quite normal."

The letter does not make it quite clear as to when the Cripple related his experience to Brother Anselm, but, from certain indications, we gather that it was two or three days later.

CHAPTER XVI

The Cripple's Vision

... IT WAS to the Cripple as if a door were being closed upon the world of sense. The white-draped coffin before him was becoming remote. He was aware of sinking away from outer things into an ineffable peace within—into a Presence that surged all round. At first he was conscious of an amazing sweetness, of Love penetrating his inmost being, of his own love meeting and mingling with that Love.

He remained resting in this peace, desiring nothing more, seeking nothing more. He waited.

Then it came. . . .

There appeared before him something so terrible, that, but for a strength which was not his own and which now came to him, his soul would have cried out for release from the sight.

It was the Crucified straining in agony on the Cross—the Body running with blood from the head and hands and feet, the face bruised and marred, every nerve quivering with pain, the whole frame racked with torture.

And this was but a part of what he saw.

There was something more; and before the terror of it the physical anguish seemed almost to pale away.

The Crucified was now immersed in a dense blackness—in the horror of a great darkness that surrounded and covered, that crushed with an overwhelming pressure. A darkness not like that of the night. An evil darkness: a vivid, living intensity of everything evil, of everything vile and unholy; malignant, vibrant through and through with hatred and malice. It enveloped the One Who hung there, isolated Him in abject loneliness, clutched Him in cruel embrace—concentrating upon His Person all the forces of Hell, all the Satanic powers, all the world's hate. There was no help, no relief from its foul, gripping fingers. The Crucified was nailed there at its mercy—and no mercy came.

It was Sin.

From out of the blackness came a cry: *Eloi, Eloi, lamma sabacthani?* And in that cry was contained the supremity of all suffering; of the God-Man's agony for man—for love of man. And no man could understand, but only God Who hung there and endured.

The Cross became clear to him once more. Beneath it were Innocente and himself. Something was happening. . . . For an infinitesimal space of time Innocente, and then himself for a longer space, were there upon the Cross, being touched with its pain—but only touched.

He understood.

It was what had happened to them. It was their share of the Cross. And it was as nought before that which he had seen.

A torrent of love swept through his being. Again he rested in that innermost peace, seeing nothing, hearing nothing—only knowing. . . .

He saw again.

A vast sphere appeared. So vast as to seem more than his vision could take in. He perceived it as being immeasurably greater than space and time, exceeding the whole natural order of things, expanding outwards and upwards until lost in fathomless heights above.

Beneath the immensity of this sphere at the centre of its curvature there was a small dark object on which the sphere seemed to rest. The dark object was not sustaining the sphere. Rather, the sphere was touching it to give access to itself; for, at the point of junction, entrance could be gained.

The understanding of it came to him.

The sphere was the Catholic Church. The dark object was the world. Its darkness was that of a heavy shadow. He saw it as the shadow of pain and suffering and sin. There was but one means of escape, one only, from the gloom and misery of it—through the entrance into the sphere. The shadow lay within the sphere as well; yet there it was different. It was luminous, like a mist through which the sun is shining. The gloom of it was gone.

He looked—and at the centre the mist was dispersing.

A glory was breaking through, piercing the obscurity, pouring forth transplendency as it came.

This glory grew, soaring downwards to the depths, upwards to the heights, and across the sphere from breadth to breadth, in the form of four great beams. It was the Cross. And on its beams was stretched the Christ—no longer veiled in darkness. The Figure was ablaze. It was Christ conquering, Christ reigning from the Cross, Christ radiating life.

For from the Cross streamed seven mighty rivers, seven rivers of life, seven rivers of grace—their waters filling the spaces of the sphere, flowing to the uttermost ends.

He saw them as the seven Sacraments of God.

And he saw the sphere in another manner now—as, in a mystical way, the Body of Christ. The vastness of it was full with living beings, members of His Body. They drank of those rivers of life. For them the Crucified had agonized; offered Himself in death—to release those seven floods, that they might drink and live.

And yet, for all the glory of the Cross, the shadow was still there within the sphere, the shadow of pain and suffering and sin; but luminous and quivering with Love. For the rivers gave release from the darkness of sin; transformed the suffering and pain for the purifying of the sufferers, drawing to the Cross all who drank, so that He Who hung there suffered with them and they with Him, He in them and they in Him. They were suffering to be made like Himself.

As he contemplated the mystery, a volume of infinite pleading seemed to be sweeping up from the Cross, carrying with it all the sufferings of Christ and His members as an intense prayer into the blazing heights of light above; and the floodgates of Divine pity opening, deluging down in torrents of love upon all who suffered and sinned, filling the sphere and overflowing upon those in the darkness of the world without—that they too might be drawn within.

So did he perceive that no suffering was lost, that pain was not in vain. So also did he perceive the reason of the sphere's magnitude, and of the world's littleness. It was the sphere that mattered: the world mattered not. It was being within the sphere that mattered—the one thing that mattered. It mattered eternally. To be without was to be away from all things; from the Cross, from the Crucified, from the Light, from the

Truth. Without was the shadow of death. Within was the grandeur of Life.

The vision of it passed.

Again he rested in that innermost peace, seeing nothing, hearing nothing—only knowing. . . .

It came.

It came as the dawn of morning, as a sun rising. It grew and increased—a flaming splendour such as no earthly day had ever known, or ever could know.

There came upon him a blindness. Three times he tried to see. Three times the blindness returned. And he knew that of himself he could not look upon that glory; that no man could.

He was still. . . .

His eyes were opened, and he saw. He saw it in imagery:

The sphere was still there, in dim outline. There was no shadow now inside to accentuate the immensity of its curve. It was all white with the whiteness of translucent light, the whiteness of that blinding splendour; all depths of crystal transparency, aglow from that which was within. For at the centre, encircled in an infinite glory of His own, was One Who had hung upon a Cross, the King of heaven and earth, Creator of all that is—the God Who was crucified by His creatures, Who gave His life to save—His hands and feet and side a blaze of glorious wounds.
. . . . . . There were Two besides. And yet the Three were One. . . .

The seven rivers flowed no more. Their work was done. The reason of it lay revealed within the sphere. Its glowing transparency was that of the mystical Body, now glorified. Its members lived no longer by the rivers, but by their oneness with Eternal Life. He, Who was in the midst, was in the whole, living within those countless millions, pervading their being through and through with His own Being as with the radiance of molten light. His light was the whiteness of the sphere, His purity its crystal clearness, His love its lambent flames.

Host upon host, legion upon legion, myriad upon myriad, they could be seen. No man could number them. From measureless spaces they gazed and loved, contemplating the Infinite. And here was a mystery: that they each of them saw Him face to face; they each possessed Him for themselves; they each knew Him as He knew them. And this not of themselves—for that were more than they could bear; but by the power He gave them.

They were absorbed; ceaselessly active. They knew no weariness; nor could they ever know it, knowing Him. They desired no more; nor could ever desire more. All they aspired to, all that they sought was there in His depthless Being. Nor could they turn away their gaze; there was nought to see but Himself. Nor sin any more, looking into Eyes as a flame of fire. They were deified, sharing His Nature by grace.

All that had been was as if it had not been. All tears had been wiped from their eyes. No suffering touched them; nothing could harm, no sorrow come, no shadow of death cross their pathway. The former things had passed away. Yet, they were glad those things had been; for thereby they were tried, and not found wanting. Thereby they were crowned with Life.

Their bodies too were glorified.

—Some had been broken and twisted; weakly, decrepit, decayed; sightless or speechless, bed-ridden, racked with disease, insane. Some had been ugly and loathsome, leprous with festering sores; or vulgar and common and dirty, reeking with vermin and filth; drunkards, gin-sodden prostitutes, drug-maniacs, criminals, thieves—they had broken from fetters of vice and shame, allured by the spell of the Cross. Some there were had been murdered—they were there with their murderers too, who in tears and Blood had found mercy, absolved at the gates of death. Some had suffered and died as babes—to be beatified, raised from the pangs of a moment to sudden, endless bliss. Some had been torn to pieces, drawn, quartered, burnt alive—all for the love of a Saviour Whom the world ever crucified. Theirs was a greater glory—their wounds were ablaze like His own.—

Their bodies were all made perfect now, aureoled with heaven's own light, resplendent with the beauty that shines from stars in the night. They could pass with the swiftness of lightning, to and fro from space to space. There was nothing to hinder or hold them, nothing to mar or maim, nothing to tarnish their glory, nothing to hurt or pain.

There were others, great hosts—His angels, ranged by celestial might, spanning the central spaces, armies on armies of light.

There was one who had stood at the foot of the Cross to be pierced by a sharp-edged sword—for giving the world a Saviour. She was crowned with a crown of twelve stars.

There was silence in heaven it seemed, for a time. . . . Then a Voice from eternity came: *I am Alpha and Omega, the Beginning and End.* It rolled from abyss to abyss. . . .

From the heights and the depths and the breadths thundered back, pealing from end to end: *Thou wast and Thou art and Thou art to come.* . . .

And everything faded away. . . .

Once more he sank into that innermost peace, seeing nothing, hearing nothing. . . .

He was coming back from some deep place, to the surface of things. The outer world was returning. . . .

The Cripple opened his eyes on a little white-draped coffin, round which the candle-flames still flickered. Someone was kneeling within the circle of their light. It was Brother Anselm.

.   .   .   .   .

At the end of his letter Brother Anselm says:

"He related the mystical experience described after I had asked him to do so, and then only with reluctance and the utmost humility. He told it all in that boyish, lovable way of his—shyly, half afraid to do so. As I listened it came to me that his love for God was a very tremendous thing. He seems, in an incredibly short time, to have been raised to a very high state of prayer. I can only account for this by supposing that his utter self-surrender has called forth rivers of grace. . . . . . .

"I have, at times, found it almost more than I could bear to look upon his broken body. I have even had to turn away from those sunken eyes, lest he should see their pathos reflected in my own; for his life is now a living death. But today, as we talked, I began to understand that his helplessness, his pain, his loss of everything are no longer his anguish, but his glory; that, although he would gladly have gone with Innocente, yet he would rather offer his living death than his life in death before the time. . . . . . .

"It is, I think, the hardest thing I have ever had to do—to let him go. And, when he has gone, I know that everything here will still speak to me of him. My very hands will ache to wheel him about once more. The trees in the garden will whisper his name; the mountains on which he was broken will ask me where he is; a little grave in their midst will recall the 'gift' that he gave. The flowers at the road-side will remind me of a withered bunch that he is taking back.

"When I am alone in the shadows of the church he will be lying there to learn the meaning of it all, beneath the Crucified. When the silence of the night descends, it will be upon his Gethsemane of

pain. Sometimes I shall see him looking upon a small still figure, silent and white, holding for the last time a pair of baby hands folded over his own crucifix.

"Yes, he means all that to me; and yet I must let him go.

"His work is not yet finished—the work he has to do. His life will be an agony, a glad agony of prayer; a work of expiation for those who libel God; a witness to Eternal love for those who doubt or fear: alone—until the day dawn, and the shadows flee away."

THE END

OTHER TITLES AVAILABLE FROM ST. AIDAN PRESS

View a sample chapter from each title at www.staidanpress.com.

THE QUEEN'S TRAGEDY
by Msgr. Robert Hugh Benson

"Upon the publication of former books of mine several kindly critics remarked that the reign of Mary Tudor told a very different story with regard to the Catholic character. It is that story which I am now attempting to set forth as honestly as I can."

$19.00 — 364 pages. Available at amazon.com.

THE NET
by Agnes Blundell

"Roger felt a freezing dew break out upon his forehead. The net was over him it seemed; in vain he told himself that he could establish his identity. His head was worth forty pounds to the vile creatures at the stair foot, and once in their clutches who knew if he could ever communicate with his friends? . . . Gaolers and pursuivants alike fattened on the traffic in human life and divided the spoils. Judges were as careless as callous."

$16.00 — 264 pages. Available at amazon.com.

THE ANCHORHOLD
by Enid Dinnis

Editha de Beauville had wealth, wit, and beauty; yet a chaplain's sermon drove her to give up the world and enter the religious life. But could a proud, strong-willed noblewoman embrace the poverty and self-abnegation, and particularly her full seclusion in an anchorhold? Read on to learn how she fared, and how her life affected those around her, including Sir Aleric, her erstwhile suitor, now a crusader knight; Fr. Nicholas, a young priest who was quite bright, and thought so, too; and Fiddlemee, the witty yet wise court jester whose past held a surprising secret.

$14.00 — 194 pages. Available at amazon.com.

THE SHEPHERD OF WEEPINGWOLD
by Enid Dinnis

Sir Robert Luffkyn, rich grandson of a peasant, has purchased the manor of Weepingwold from the noble but impoverished de Lessels, intending to make the renamed Luffkynwold a busy center of his tanning trade. He sends Petronilla, last de Lessels, to Gracerood, intending her for its future Abbess, and plucks little Brother Kit from the cloister to become the new parson of the long-abandoned church. How will Father Kit fare with the parish and his own soul? What is Petronilla's true vocation? And is there really a witch in the parish?

$14.00 — 202 pages. Available at amazon.com.

SCOUTING FOR SECRET SERVICE
by Fr. Bernard F. J. Dooley

Frank and George are going to spend their summer vacation in the Adirondacks, thanks to Frank's uncle Ed. But once they get there, they realize something fishy is going on. Can they trust Pete, their Indian guide, or is he mixed up in it too? And is Frank's mysterious uncle really behind it all?

$14.00 — 188 pages. Available at amazon.com.

CANDLELIGHT ATTIC AND ODD JOB'S
by Cecily Hallack

Here are seven true stories in honour of the Seven Joys of Our Blessed Lady, and ten more invented ones about the delightful Barnabas Job, to make a comfortable book for those who are afraid of the dark.

$14.00 — 192 pages. Available at amazon.com.

THE HAPPINESS OF FATHER HAPPÉ
by Cecily Hallack

Shingle Bay did not know what to make of Fr. Savinius Happé. He was a cheerful, rotund Franciscan, a famous author of books on everything from Etruscan civilization to Alpine meadows to beetles, and someone who had never quite mastered the English language. His jovial demeanor concealed a wisdom that alternately bewildered, astonished, but ultimately won over the people of Shingle Bay.

$10.00 — 112 pages. Available at amazon.com.

CON OF MISTY MOUNTAIN
by Mary T. Waggaman

"It had been a long night for Con. Just what had happened to him he was at first too dazed to know. Dennis had flung him into the smoking-room with no very gentle hand, turned the key and left him to himself. And, sinking down dully upon a rug that felt very soft and warm after the hard flight over the mountain, Con was glad to rest his bruised, aching limbs, his dizzy head, without any thought of what was to come upon him next."

$14.00 — 190 pages. Available at www.amazon.com.

NON-FICTION

CATHOLICISM AND SCOTLAND
by Compton Mackenzie

Much has been written about the desperate fight that English Catholics waged to keep the Faith, but Scotland's Catholic history is little known. Have you ever heard of David Beaton, Cardinal Archbishop of St. Andrews, and his struggles? Or of Fr. Ninian Winzet, who boldly challenged Calvinist champion John Knox to a public debate? Read this book and find out about the Scots who sought to defend their country and their Faith from the onslaught of Protestantism.

$12.00 — 138 pages. Available at amazon.com.